# WEYGANDT: ACCOUNTING PRINCIPLES, 4th CANADIAN EDITION, PART 2
# CHAPTER 8: ACCOUNTING FOR RECEIVABLES

A Wiley Canada Custom Publication for

## Seneca College

## Acc 120

*Wiley Canada Custom Services*
JOHN WILEY & SONS CANADA, LTD.

Cover Photo Credit: Interrobang Graphic Design

Printed and bound in Canada
10 9 8 7 6 5 4 3 2 1

John Wiley & Sons Canada, Ltd
6045 Freemont Blvd.
Mississauga, Ontario
L5R 4J3
Visit our website at: www.wiley.ca

**FOURTH CANADIAN EDITION**

# ACCOUNTING

# PRINCIPLES

▶ **Jerry J. Weygandt**   *Ph.D., C.P.A.*

Arthur Andersen Alumni Professor of Accounting
University of Wisconsin – Madison

▶ **Donald E. Kieso**   *Ph.D., C.P.A.*

KPMG Peat Marwick Emeritus Professor of Accounting
Northern Illinois University

▶ **Paul D. Kimmel**   *Ph.D., C.P.A.*

University of Wisconsin – Milwaukee

▶ **Barbara Trenholm**   *M.B.A., F.C.A.*

University of New Brunswick – Fredericton

▶ **Valerie A. Kinnear**   *M.Sc. (Bus. Admin.), C.A.*

Mount Royal College

**John Wiley & Sons Canada, Ltd.**

*To our students — past, present, and future*

**Library and Archives Canada Cataloguing in Publication**

Accounting principles / Jerry J. Weygandt ... [et al.].

4th Canadian ed.

Includes index.

ISBN 978-0-470-83858-7 (pt. 1)
ISBN 978-0-470-83860-0 (pt. 2)
ISBN 978-0-470-83861-7 (pt. 3)

1. Accounting--Textbooks.  I. Weygandt, Jerry J.

HF5635.A3778 2006          657'.044          C2006-906471-7

**Production Credits**

Editorial Manager: Karen Staudinger
Publishing Services Director: Karen Bryan
Media Editor: Elsa Passera Berardi
Editorial Assistant: Sheri Coombs
Director of Marketing: Isabelle Moreau
Design & Typesetting: OrangeSprocket Communications
Cover Design: Interrobang Graphic Design
Bicentennial Logo Design: Richard J. Pacifico
Printing & Binding: Quebecor World Inc.

Printed and bound in the United States
1 2 3 4 5 QW 11 10 09 08 07

John Wiley & Sons Canada, Ltd.
6045 Freemont Blvd.
Mississauga, Ontario L5R 4J3
Visit our website at: www.wiley.ca

## concepts for review >>

Before studying this chapter, you should understand or, if necessary, review:

  a. How to record revenue. (Ch. 3, pp. 106–107 and Ch. 5, pp. 231–234)

  b. Why adjusting entries are made. (Ch. 3, pp. 108–109)

  c. How to calculate interest. (Ch. 3, p. 117)

the navigator

# Personal Touch Helps Keep Receivables Healthy

*Whitehill Technologies: www.whitehilltech.com*

MONCTON, N.B.—Since its founding in 1997, Whitehill Technologies has grown from just two employees to a staff of more than 100 and annual sales of more than $11 million. Today, the company's software—which enables companies in the financial services, legal, and insurance sectors to create business documents from data stored on older systems—is used by nearly 700 clients in 45 countries.

Whitehill's revenue comes from software licence sales, services such as installation, training, and template customization, and ongoing maintenance. The company usually has about $2.5 million in accounts receivable at any time.

"We bill for licence fees up front—they're due upon receipt—and our regular terms for services and maintenance are n/30," explains Paul Gunn, Whitehill's VP of Finance and Administration. "With our resellers, it's a little different—we have some that settle quarterly and others that settle monthly."

Contrary to some large companies, Whitehill does not charge interest for amounts past due; nor does it offer discounts for early payment. As Mr. Gunn points out, the fact that the company has "the ability to cut off support" is usually enough to encourage payment on time.

The company uses a weekly aging report to keep track of its receivables. "When an invoice is nearing 30 days, we will initiate contact with the client, usually by telephone or e-mail to make sure it's in their system," explains Mr. Gunn. "If it gets on to 45 days, we would talk with our project manager and look for an additional contact in the organization."

An account over 90 days goes on a red flag list. "At that point, senior management would likely get involved," says Mr. Gunn. But by keeping personal contact every step of the way, he adds, the company usually gets customers to pay long before that happens. Still, the company records an estimate for bad debts every year.

"When Whitehill was starting out and growing, accounts receivable collections provided our lifeblood (cash)," says Mr. Gunn. "As we have grown and become stronger financially, we've continued to manage our receivables with the same level of diligence and attention." With receivables, the key is to stay on top of them at all times by having a process for dealing with them at whatever stage they're at.

the navigator

## chapter 8

# Accounting for Receivables

## study objectives >>

the navigator

After studying this chapter, you should be able to:

1. Record accounts receivable transactions.
2. Calculate the net realizable value of accounts receivable and account for bad debts.
3. Account for notes receivable.
4. Demonstrate the presentation, analysis, and management of receivables.

As indicated in our feature story, management of receivables is important for any company that sells on credit, as Whitehill Technologies does. In this chapter, we will first review the journal entries that companies make when goods and services are sold on account and when cash is collected from those sales. Next, we will learn how companies estimate, record, and then, in some cases, collect their uncollectible accounts. We will also learn about notes receivable.

The chapter is organized as follows:

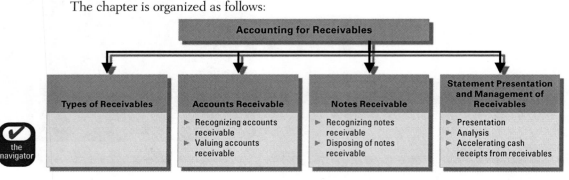

# Types of Receivables

The term "receivables" refers to amounts due from individuals and other companies. They are claims that are expected to be collected in cash. The two most common types of receivables are accounts receivable and notes receivable.

**Accounts receivable** are amounts owed by customers on account. They result from the sale of goods and services. These receivables are generally expected to be collected within 30 days or so, and are classified as current assets. They are usually the most significant type of claim held by a company.

**Notes receivable** are claims for which formal instruments of credit are issued as proof of the debt. A note normally requires the debtor to pay interest and extends for periods of 30 days or longer. Notes receivable may be either current assets or long-term assets, depending on their due dates. Notes and accounts receivable that result from sale transactions are often called **trade receivables**.

Other receivables include interest receivable, loans or advances to employees, and recoverable sales and income taxes. These receivables are generally classified and reported as separate items in the current or noncurrent sections of the balance sheet, according to their due dates.

# Accounts Receivable

Two important accounting issues for accounts receivable—recognizing accounts receivable and valuing accounts receivable—will be discussed in this section. A third issue—accelerating cash receipts from receivables—is discussed later in the chapter.

## Recognizing Accounts Receivable

**study objective 1**

Record accounts receivable transactions.

Recognizing accounts receivable is relatively straightforward. For a service company, a receivable is recorded when the service is provided on account. For a merchandising company, a receivable is recorded at the point of sale of merchandise on account. Recall that in Chapter 5 we also saw how accounts receivable are reduced by sales returns and allowances and sales discounts.

To review, assume that Adorable Junior Garment sells merchandise on account to Zellers on July 1 for $1,000 with payment terms of 2/10, n/30. On July 4, Zellers returns merchandise worth $100 to Adorable Junior Garment. On July 10, Adorable Junior Garment receives payment from Zellers for the balance due. Assume Adorable Junior Garment uses a periodic inventory system. The journal entries to record these transactions on the books of Adorable Junior Garment are as follows:

| July 1 | Accounts Receivable—Zellers | 1,000 | |
| | Sales | | 1,000 |
| | To record sale of merchandise on account. | | |
| 4 | Sales Returns and Allowances | 100 | |
| | Accounts Receivable—Zellers | | 100 |
| | To record merchandise returned. | | |
| 10 | Cash [($1,000 − $100) × 98%] | 882 | |
| | Sales Discounts [($1,000 − $100) × 2%] | 18 | |
| | Accounts Receivable—Zellers | | 900 |
| | To record collection of accounts receivable. | | |

| A | = | L | + | OE |
|---|---|---|---|---|
| +1,000 | | | | +1,000 |

Cash flows: no effect

| A | = | L | + | OE |
|---|---|---|---|---|
| −100 | | | | −100 |

Cash flows: no effect

| A | = | L | + | OE |
|---|---|---|---|---|
| +882 | | | | −18 |
| −900 | | | | |

↑ Cash flows: +882

If Adorable Junior Garment used a perpetual inventory system, a second journal entry to record the cost of the goods sold (and the cost of the goods returned) would be required for the July 1 and July 4 transactions.

## Subsidiary Accounts Receivable Ledger

Adorable Junior Garment does not have only Zellers as a customer. It has hundreds of customers. If it recorded the accounts receivable for each of these customers in only one general ledger account, as we did above in Accounts Receivable, it would be hard to determine the balance owed by a specific customer, such as Zellers, at a specific point in time.

Instead, most companies that sell on account use a subsidiary ledger to keep track of individual customer accounts. As we learned in Chapter 5, a subsidiary ledger gives supporting detail to the general ledger. Illustration 8-1 on the next page shows an accounts receivable control account and subsidiary ledger, using assumed data.

Each entry that affects accounts receivable is basically posted twice—once to the subsidiary ledger and once to the general ledger. Normally entries to the subsidiary ledger are posted daily, while entries to the general ledger are summarized and posted monthly. For example, the $1,000 sale to Zellers was posted to Zellers' account in the subsidiary ledger on July 1. It was also summarized with other sales entries (Kids Online $6,000 + Snazzy Kids $3,000 + Zellers $1,000 = $10,000) in a special sales journal and posted to the accounts receivable control account in the general ledger at the end of the month, on July 31.

Collections on account (Kids Online $4,000 + Snazzy Kids $1,000 + Zellers $900 = $5,900) were also posted individually to the subsidiary ledger accounts and summarized and posted in total to the general ledger account. Non-recurring entries, such as the sales return of $100, are posted to both the subsidiary and general ledgers individually.

Note that the balance of $4,000 in the control account agrees with the total of the balances in the individual accounts receivable accounts in the subsidiary ledger (Kids Online $2,000 + Snazzy Kids $2,000 + Zellers $0). There is more information about how subsidiary ledgers work in Appendix C at the end of this textbook.

**Illustration 8-1 ▶**

Accounts receivable general ledger control account and subsidiary ledger

| GENERAL LEDGER | | | | | |
|---|---|---|---|---|---|
| Accounts Receivable is a control account. | Accounts Receivable | | | | No. 112 |
| Date | Explanation | Ref. | Debit | Credit | Balance |
| 2007 July 4 | | | | 100 | (100) |
| 31 | | | 10,000 | | 9,900 |
| 31 | | | | 5,900 | 4,000 |

| ACCOUNTS RECEIVABLE SUBSIDIARY LEDGER | | | | | |
|---|---|---|---|---|---|
| The subsidiary ledger is separate from the general ledger. | Kids Online | | | | No. 112-203 |
| Date | Explanation | Ref. | Debit | Credit | Balance |
| 2007 July 11 | Invoice 1310 | | 6,000 | | 6,000 |
| 19 | Payment | | | 4,000 | 2,000 |

| | Snazzy Kids Co. | | | | No. 112-413 |
|---|---|---|---|---|---|
| Date | Explanation | Ref. | Debit | Credit | Balance |
| 2007 July 12 | Invoice 1318 | | 3,000 | | 3,000 |
| 21 | Payment | | | 1,000 | 2,000 |

| | Zellers Inc. | | | | No. 112-581 |
|---|---|---|---|---|---|
| Date | Explanation | Ref. | Debit | Credit | Balance |
| 2007 July 1 | Invoice 1215 | | 1,000 | | 1,000 |
| 4 | Credit memo 1222 | | | 100 | 900 |
| 10 | Payment | | | 900 | 0 |

## Interest Revenue

At the end of each month, the company can use the subsidiary ledger to easily determine the transactions that occurred in each customer's account during the month and then send the customer a statement of transactions for the month. If the customer does not pay in full within a specified period (usually 30 days), most retailers add an interest (financing) charge to the balance due. Interest rates vary from company to company, but rates for retailers can be as high as 28.8 percent per year.

When financing charges are added, the seller recognizes interest revenue. If Kids Online still owes $2,000 at the end of the next month, August 31, and Adorable Junior Garment charges 18 percent on the balance due, the entry that Adorable Junior Garment will make to record interest revenue of $30 ($2,000 × 18% × $\frac{1}{12}$) is as follows:

| A | = | L | + | OE |
|---|---|---|---|---|
| +30 | | | | +30 |

Cash flows: no effect

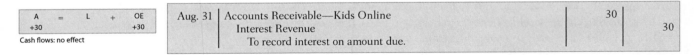

| Aug. 31 | Accounts Receivable—Kids Online | 30 | |
|---|---|---|---|
| | Interest Revenue | | 30 |
| | To record interest on amount due. | | |

Although Whitehill Technologies in our feature story does not charge interest on its overdue accounts, interest revenue is often a significant amount for service and merchandising companies. As discussed in Chapter 5, interest revenue is included in other revenues in the non-operating section of the income statement.

## Nonbank Credit Card Sales

In Chapter 7, we learned that debit and bank credit card sales are cash sales. Sales on credit cards that are not directly associated with a bank are reported as credit sales, not cash sales. Nonbank credit card sales result in an account receivable until the credit card company pays the amount owing to the seller.

To illustrate, assume that Kerr Music accepts a nonbank credit card on October 24 for a $500 bill. The entry for the sale by Kerr Music (assuming a 4% service fee) is:

| Oct. 24 | Accounts Receivable—Credit Card Company | 480 | |
| | Credit Card Expense ($500 × 4%) | 20 | |
| | Sales | | 500 |
| | To record nonbank credit card sale. | | |

| A | = | L | + | OE |
|---|---|---|---|---|
| +480 | | | | −20 |
| | | | | +500 |

Cash flows: no effect

When cash is received from the credit card company, Kerr Music will record this entry:

| Nov. 7 | Cash | 480 | |
| | Accounts Receivable—Credit Card Company | | 480 |
| | To record redemption of credit card billing. | | |

| A | = | L | + | OE |
|---|---|---|---|---|
| +480 | | | | |
| −480 | | | | |

⬆ Cash flows: +480

Advances in technology have created a rapidly changing credit card environment. Transactions and payments can be processed much more quickly, and often electronically, which reduces the time to collect cash from the credit card company. As collection time becomes shorter, credit card transactions are becoming more like cash transactions to the business.

How does a business know if it should debit Cash or Accounts Receivable when it processes a credit card transaction? Basically, it should consider how long it takes to collect the cash. If it takes longer than a few days to process the transaction and collect the cash, it should be treated as a credit sale as shown above.

Company credit cards, such as Petro-Canada and Canadian Tire, are always recorded as credit sales. When the credit card transaction results in an account receivable from the customer—as opposed to from the credit card company as shown above—the accounting treatment is the same as we have previously seen for accounts receivable.

Credit card expenses, along with debit cards expenses discussed in Chapter 7, are reported as an operating expense in the income statement.

### ACCOUNTING IN ACTION ▶ Business Insight

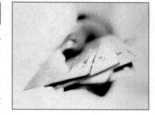

The average interest rate on a bank credit card in Canada is 18 percent. Interest on non-bank cards, such as Petro-Canada, can be as high as 28.8 percent. The Bank of Canada interest rate is 4.5 percent. Why are credit card rates so much higher than other interest rates?

The Bank of Canada interest rate is called the "risk-free" rate. This means that, theoretically, money can be borrowed at 4.5 percent if there is no other credit risk. The difference between the Bank of Canada rate and credit card rates is called a "risk premium." Banks justify this higher interest rate by saying that credit cards are a greater risk. They argue that they have to cover their losses from fraud as well as their administrative costs.

**?** Since the interest rates on company credit cards are so high, why don't all companies have their own credit cards?

## BEFORE YOU GO ON . . .

### ▶Review It

1. The stores that form the Forzani Group do not have their own company credit cards. Customers use cash, debit cards, or bank credit cards to pay for merchandise. Why then does the company report accounts receivable on its balance sheet? (*Hint:* See Note 2(h) on Revenue Recognition.) The answer to this question is at the end of the chapter.
2. What are the similarities and differences between a general ledger and a subsidiary ledger?
3. How is interest revenue calculated and recorded on late accounts receivable?
4. What are the differences between bank credit cards and nonbank credit cards?

### ▶Do It

Information for Kinholm Company follows for its first month of operations:

| Credit Sales | | | Cash Collections | | |
|---|---|---|---|---|---|
| Jan. 5 | Sych Co. | $12,000 | Jan. 16 | Sych Co. | $9,000 |
| 9 | Downey Inc. | 5,000 | 22 | Downey Inc. | 3,500 |
| 13 | Pawlak Co. | 6,000 | 28 | Pawlak Co. | 6,000 |

Calculate (a) the balances that appear in the accounts receivable subsidiary ledger for each customer, and (b) the accounts receivable balance that appears in the general ledger at the end of January.

### Action Plan

- Use T accounts as a simple method of calculating account balances.
- Create separate accounts for each customer and post their transactions to their accounts.
- Create one account for the Accounts Receivable control account.
- Post the total credit sales and the total cash collections to the general ledger.

### Solution

**ACCOUNTS RECEIVABLE SUBSIDIARY LEDGER**

Sych Co.

| Jan. 5 | 12,000 | Jan. 16 | 9,000 |
|---|---|---|---|
| Bal. | 3,000 | | |

Downey Inc.

| Jan. 9 | 5,000 | Jan. 22 | 3,500 |
|---|---|---|---|
| Bal. | 1,500 | | |

Pawlak Co.

| Jan. 13 | 6,000 | Jan. 28 | 6,000 |
|---|---|---|---|
| Bal. | 0 | | |

**GENERAL LEDGER**

Accounts Receivable

| Jan. 31 | 23,000[a] | Jan. 31 | 18,500[b] |
|---|---|---|---|
| Bal. | 4,500 | | |

[a] $12,000 + $5,000 + $6,000 = $23,000
[b] $9,000 + $3,500 + $6,000 = $18,500

the navigator

*Related exercise material:* BE8–1, BE8–2, BE8–3, BE8–4, E8–1, E8–2, and E8–3.

# Valuing Accounts Receivable

After receivables are recorded in the accounts, the next question is how these receivables should be reported on the balance sheet. Receivables are assets, but determining the amount to report as an asset is sometimes difficult because some receivables will become uncollectible. A receivable can only be reported as an asset if it will give a future benefit. This means that only collectible receivables can be reported as assets in the financial statements. This collectible amount is called the **net realizable value** of the receivables.

Whitehill Technologies in our feature story works closely with customers to collect its receivables. But even if each of Whitehill's customers satisfied Whitehill's credit requirements before the credit sale was approved, inevitably, some accounts receivable become uncollectible. For example, a usually reliable customer may suddenly not be able to pay because of an unexpected decrease in its revenues or because it is faced with unexpected bills.

You might be wondering why a company would sell goods or services on credit if there is a risk of not collecting the receivable. These companies are expecting that the increase in revenues and profit from selling on credit will be greater than any uncollectible accounts or credit losses. Such losses are considered a normal and necessary risk of doing business on a credit basis.

When receivables are written down to their net realizable value because of credit losses, owner's equity must also be reduced. This is done by recording an expense, known as **bad debts expense**, for the credit losses. The key issue in valuing accounts receivable is when to record these credit losses. If the company waits until it knows for sure that the specific account will not be collected, it could end up recording the bad debts expense in a different period than when the revenue is recorded.

**Helpful hint** Bad debts expense is also sometimes called *uncollectible account expense*.

Consider the following example. Assume that in 2007 Quick Buck Computer Company decides it could increase its revenues by offering computers to students without requiring any money down and with no credit approval process. On campuses across the country, it sells one million computers with a selling price of $700 each. This increases Quick Buck's revenues and receivables by $700 million. The promotion is a huge success! The 2007 balance sheet and income statement look great. Unfortunately, in 2008, nearly 40 percent of the student customers default on their accounts. This makes the year 2008 income statement and balance sheet look terrible. Illustration 8-2 shows that the promotion in 2007 was not such a great success after all.

**Year 2007**

Huge sales promotion.
Sales increase dramatically.
Accounts receivable increase dramatically.

**Year 2008**

Customers default on loans.
Bad debts expense increases dramatically.
Accounts receivable drop dramatically.

**Illustration 8-2 ◀**

Effects of mismatching bad debts

If credit losses are not recorded until they occur, bad debts expense is not matched to sales revenues in the income statement. Recall that the matching principle requires expenses to be recorded in the same period as the sales they helped generate. Quick Buck Computer Company's income was overstated in 2007 and understated in 2008 because we did not match the bad debts expense with sales revenue.

In addition, the accounts receivable in the balance sheet are not reported at the amount that is actually expected to be received. Consequently, Quick Buck Computer's receivables are overstated at the end of 2007, which misrepresents the amount that should have been reported as an asset.

To avoid this mismatch, we therefore cannot wait until we know exactly which receivables are uncollectible. Instead, in the accounting period where the sales occur, we must estimate the uncollectible accounts receivable. Because we do not know which specific accounts receivable will need to be written off, we use what is known as the allowance method.

The **allowance method** of accounting for bad debts estimates uncollectible accounts at the end of each accounting period. This gives better matching of expenses with revenues on the income statement because credit losses that are expected to happen from sales or service revenue in that accounting period are recorded in the same accounting period as when the revenue was earned. It also ensures that receivables are stated at their net realizable value on the balance sheet. It removes the amounts that the company estimates it will not collect.

The allowance method is required for financial reporting purposes when bad debts are material (significant) in amount. It has three essential features:

1. Recording estimated uncollectibles: The amount of uncollectible accounts receivable is estimated at the end of the accounting period. This estimate is treated as bad debts expense and is matched against revenues in the accounting period where the revenues are recorded.
2. Recording the write-off of an uncollectible account: Actual uncollectibles are written off when the specific account is determined to be uncollectible.
3. Recovery of an uncollectible account: When an account that was previously written off is later collected, the original write-off is reversed and the collection is recorded.

We will see that neither the write-off nor the later recovery affect the income statement, and matching is therefore not affected by the timing of these entries.

## 1. Recording Estimated Uncollectibles

To illustrate the allowance method, assume that Adorable Junior Garment has net credit sales of $1.2 million in 2007. Of this amount, $200,000 remains uncollected at December 31. The credit manager estimates (using techniques we will discuss in the next section) that $24,000 of these receivables will be uncollectible. The adjusting entry to record the estimated uncollectible accounts is:

| A | = | L | + | OE |
|---|---|---|---|---|
| −24,000 | | | | −24,000 |

Cash flows: no effect

| Dec. 31 | Bad Debts Expense | 24,000 | |
|---------|-------------------|--------|--------|
| | Allowance for Doubtful Accounts | | 24,000 |
| | To record estimate of uncollectible accounts. | | |

Note that Bad Debts Expense is used, instead of debiting a contra sales account, as we did for sales returns and allowances. An expense account is used because the responsibilities for granting credit and collecting accounts are normally separated from sales and marketing. Bad Debts Expense is reported in the income statement as an operating expense. The estimated uncollectibles are matched with sales in 2007 because the expense is recorded in the year when the sales are made.

Also note that Allowance for Doubtful Accounts—a contra asset account—is used instead of a direct credit to Accounts Receivable. As mentioned earlier, this is mainly because we do not know which individual customers will not pay. We do not know which specific accounts to credit in the subsidiary ledger. Recall that subsidiary ledger accounts must balance with Accounts Receivable, the control account. This would not happen if the control account was credited and the subsidiary ledger accounts were not. Also, the estimate for uncollectibles is just an estimate. A contra account helps to separate estimates from actual amounts, such as those found in Accounts Receivable.

The account balance in Allowance for Doubtful Accounts is deducted from Accounts Receivable in the current assets section of the balance sheet. Assuming that Adorable Junior Garment has an unadjusted balance of $1,000 in Allowance for Doubtful Accounts, its ending balance of $25,000 ($1,000 + $24,000) would be reported as follows:

| ADORABLE JUNIOR GARMENT | | |
|---|---|---|
| Balance Sheet (partial) | | |
| December 31, 2007 | | |
| Current assets | | |
| Cash | | $ 14,800 |
| Accounts receivable | $200,000 | |
| Less: Allowance for doubtful accounts | 25,000 | 175,000 |
| Merchandise inventory | | 310,000 |
| Prepaid expenses | | 25,000 |
| Total current assets | | 524,800 |

The $25,000 in Allowance for Doubtful Accounts shows the receivables that are expected to become uncollectible in the future. The amount $175,000 is the expected net realizable value of the accounts receivable at the statement date. The $175,000 is added to cash, merchandise inventory, and prepaid expenses to calculate total current assets, and not the total accounts receivable.

The net realizable value can be presented by the formula shown in Illustration 8-3.

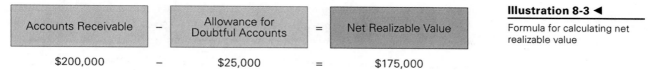

| Accounts Receivable | − | Allowance for Doubtful Accounts | = | Net Realizable Value |
|---|---|---|---|---|
| $200,000 | − | $25,000 | = | $175,000 |

**Illustration 8-3 ◀**

Formula for calculating net realizable value

**Estimating the Allowance.** For Adorable Junior Garment, the amount of the expected bad debts expense in the journal entry on the previous page ($24,000) was given. But how was this estimate calculated? There are two approaches that most companies use to determine this amount: (1) percentage of sales, and (2) percentage of receivables.

**Percentage of Sales Approach.** The **percentage of sales approach** calculates bad debts expense as a percentage of net credit sales. Management determines the percentage based on past experience and the company's credit policy.

To illustrate, assume that Adorable Junior Garment decides to use the percentage of sales approach. It concludes that 2 percent of net credit sales will become uncollectible. Recall that net credit sales for the calendar year 2007 are $1.2 million. The estimated bad debts expense is $24,000 (2% × $1,200,000). The adjusting entry is:

| Dec. 31 | Bad Debts Expense | 24,000 | |
|---|---|---|---|
| | Allowance for Doubtful Accounts | | 24,000 |
| | To record estimate of bad debts expense. | | |

| A | = | L | + | OE |
|---|---|---|---|---|
| −24,000 | | | | −24,000 |

Cash flows: no effect

Recall that Allowance for Doubtful Accounts had a credit balance of $1,000 before the adjustment. After the adjusting entry is posted, the accounts will show the following:

| Bad Debts Expense | | Allowance for Doubtful Accounts | |
|---|---|---|---|
| Dec. 31 Adj. 24,000 | | Dec. 31 Bal. 1,000 | |
| | | 31 Adj. 24,000 | |
| | | Dec. 31 Bal. 25,000 | |

**Helpful hint** Because the income statement is emphasized in the percentage of sales approach, the balance in the allowance account is not involved in calculating the bad debts expense in the adjusting entry.

When calculating the amount in the adjusting entry ($24,000), the existing balance in Allowance for Doubtful Accounts is ignored. But after posting the adjusting entry, the balance in Allowance for Doubtful Accounts should be a reasonable approximation of the uncollectible accounts receivable. If actual write-offs in the next year are very different from the amount that was estimated, a different percentage should be used in calculating the adjusting entry in future years.

This approach to estimating uncollectibles results in an excellent matching of expenses with revenues because the bad debts expense is related to the sales recorded in the same period. Because an income statement account (Sales) is used to calculate another income statement account (Bad Debts Expense), and any balance in the balance sheet account (Allowance for Doubtful Accounts) is ignored, this approach is often called the **income statement approach**.

The percentage of sales approach is quick and easy to use. This is why it is often used to update bad debts for interim reports.

*Percentage of Receivables Approach.* Under the **percentage of receivables approach**, management uses past experience to estimate the percentage of receivables that will become uncollectible accounts. The easiest way to do this is to multiply the total amount of accounts receivable by a percentage based on an overall estimate of the total uncollectible accounts.

Another way to calculate uncollectible accounts is to use different percentages depending on how long the accounts receivable have been outstanding. This way is more sensitive to the actual status of the accounts receivable. A schedule must be prepared, called an **aging schedule**, which shows the age of each account receivable. The longer a receivable is past due or outstanding, the less likely it is to be collected. The estimated percentage of uncollectible accounts therefore increases as the number of days outstanding increases.

After the ages of the different accounts receivable are determined, the loss from uncollectible accounts is estimated. This is done by applying percentages, based on past experience, to the totals in each category. An aging schedule for Adorable Junior Garment is shown in Illustration 8-4.

**Illustration 8-4 ▶**

Aging schedule

| Customer | Total | Number of Days Outstanding | | | | |
|---|---|---|---|---|---|---|
| | | 0–30 | 31–60 | 61–90 | 91–120 | Over 120 |
| Bansal Garments | $ 6,000 | | $ 3,000 | $ 3,000 | | |
| Bortz Clothing | 3,000 | $ 3,000 | | | | |
| Kids Online | 4,500 | | | | $ 2,000 | $ 2,500 |
| Snazzy Kids Co. | 17,000 | 2,000 | 5,000 | 5,000 | 5,000 | |
| Tykes n' Tots | 26,500 | 10,000 | 10,000 | 6,000 | 500 | |
| Zellers | 42,000 | 32,000 | 10,000 | | | |
| Wal-Mart | 61,000 | 48,000 | 12,000 | 1,000 | | |
| Others | 40,000 | 5,000 | 10,000 | 10,000 | 5,000 | 10,000 |
| | $200,000 | $100,000 | $50,000 | $25,000 | $12,500 | $12,500 |
| Estimated percentage uncollectible | | 5% | 10% | 20% | 30% | 50% |
| Estimated uncollectible accounts | $ 25,000 | $ 5,000 | $ 5,000 | $ 5,000 | $ 3,750 | $ 6,250 |

Note the increasing percentages from 5 percent to 50 percent. This percentage increase shows that there is more concern about an account being uncollectible as it gets older. We also saw this with Whitehill in our feature story. Whitehill puts accounts over 90 days on its "red flag list" and usually gets senior management involved in helping collect the account at that point.

The $25,000 total for Adorable Junior Garment's estimated uncollectible accounts is the amount of existing receivables that are expected to become uncollectible in the future. This amount is therefore the required balance in Allowance for Doubtful Accounts at the balance sheet date. The amount of the bad debts expense adjusting entry is the difference between the required balance and the existing balance in the allowance account. When using the percentage of receivables approach, the balance in the allowance account cannot be ignored.

If the trial balance shows Allowance for Doubtful Accounts with a credit balance of $1,000, an adjusting entry for $24,000 ($25,000 − $1,000) is necessary, as follows:

**Helpful hint** Because the balance sheet is emphasized in the percentage of receivables approach, the existing balance in the allowance account must be considered when calculating the bad debts expense in the adjusting entry.

| Dec. 31 | Bad Debts Expense | 24,000 | |
| | Allowance for Doubtful Accounts | | 24,000 |
| | To adjust allowance account to total estimated uncollectibles. | | |

| A | = | L | + | OE |
|---|---|---|---|---|
| −24,000 | | | | −24,000 |

Cash flows: no effect

After the adjusting entry is posted, Adorable Junior Garment's accounts will show the following:

| Bad Debts Expense | | Allowance for Doubtful Accounts | |
|---|---|---|---|
| Dec. 31 Adj.   24,000 | | Dec. 31 Bal.   1,000 | |
| | | 31 Adj.   24,000 | |
| | | Dec. 31 Bal.   25,000 | |

Occasionally, the allowance account will have a debit balance before recording the adjusting entry. This happens when write-offs in the year are higher than the previous estimates for bad debts (we will discuss write-offs in the next section). If there is debit balance, prior to recording the adjusting entry, the debit balance is added to the required balance when the adjusting entry is made. If there had been a $500 debit balance in the Adorable Junior Garment allowance account before adjustment, the adjusting entry would have been for $25,500 to arrive at a credit balance in the allowance account of $25,000.

An aging schedule, rather than a percentage of total receivables, is normally used in this approach. An aging schedule can be easily obtained from a computerized accounts receivable system. While preparing this schedule by hand takes a lot of time, the schedule can be done in minutes on a computer. Most companies have aging schedules prepared already, as this helps them closely monitor the age of their receivables. As noted in our feature story, Whitehill Technologies prepares an aging schedule every week to closely monitor how collectible its accounts receivable are and to identify problem accounts.

Whether it is done with an aging schedule or a percentage of total receivables, the percentage of receivables approach normally gives a better estimate of the net realizable value of the accounts receivable than does the percentage of sales approach. But the percentage of receivables approach does not do as good a job as the percentage of sales approach in matching bad debts expense to the period in which the sale takes place. Because a balance sheet account (Accounts Receivable) is used to calculate the required balance in another balance sheet account (Allowance for Doubtful Accounts), the percentage of receivables approach is also often called the **balance sheet approach**.

Both the percentage of sales and the percentage of receivables approaches are generally accepted. The choice is a management decision. It depends on how much emphasis management wishes to give to matching expenses and revenues on the one hand, and to the net realizable value of the accounts receivable on the other. Most companies prefer using the percentage of receivables approach. Illustration 8-5 compares the two approaches.

**Illustration 8-5 ▶**

Comparison of approaches for estimating uncollectibles

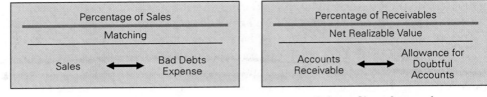

| **Income Statement Approach** | **Balance Sheet Approach** |

Under both approaches, it is necessary to review the company's past experience with credit losses. It also should be noted that, unlike in our example with Adorable Junior Garment, the two approaches normally result in different amounts in the adjusting entry.

## 2. Recording the Write-Off of an Uncollectible Account

Companies use various methods for collecting past-due accounts, including letters, calls, and legal actions. In the feature story, Whitehill Technologies uses both e-mail and telephone calls to follow up accounts that are overdue. Whitehill's senior management gets involved if an account is 90 days overdue, and the company does not hesitate to cut off technical support in order to encourage payment.

When all the ways of collecting a past-due account have been tried and collection appears impossible, the account should be written off. To prevent premature write-offs, each write-off should be approved in writing by management. To keep good internal control, the authorization to write off accounts should not be given to someone who also has responsibilities related to cash or receivables.

To illustrate a receivables write-off, assume that the vice-president of finance of Adorable Junior Garment authorizes the write-off of a $4,500 balance owed by a delinquent customer, Kids Online, on March 1, 2008. The entry to record the write-off is as follows:

| A | = | L | + | OE |
|---|---|---|---|---|
| +4,500 | | | | |
| −4,500 | | | | |

Cash flows: no effect

| Mar. 1 | Allowance for Doubtful Accounts | 4,500 | |
| | Accounts Receivable—Kids Online | | 4,500 |
| | Write-off of uncollectible account. | | |

Bad Debts Expense is not increased (debited) when the write-off occurs. Under the allowance method, every account write-off is debited to the allowance account rather than to Bad Debts Expense. A debit to Bad Debts Expense would be incorrect because the expense was already recognized when the adjusting entry was made for estimated bad debts last year.

Instead, the entry to record the write-off of an uncollectible account reduces both Accounts Receivable and Allowance for Doubtful Accounts. After posting, using an assumed balance of $230,000 in Accounts Receivable on February 29, 2008, the general ledger accounts will appear as follows:

| Accounts Receivable | | | | Allowance for Doubtful Accounts | | | |
|---|---|---|---|---|---|---|---|
| Feb. 29 Bal. | 230,000 | Mar. 1 | 4,500 | Mar. 1 | 4,500 | Jan. 1 Bal. | 25,000 |
| Mar. 1 Bal. | 225,500 | | | | | Mar. 1 Bal. | 20,500 |

A write-off affects only balance sheet accounts. The write-off of the account reduces both Accounts Receivable and Allowance for Doubtful Accounts. Net realizable value in the balance sheet remains the same, as shown below:

| | Before Write-Off | After Write-Off |
|---|---|---|
| Accounts receivable | $230,000 | $225,500 |
| Less: Allowance for doubtful accounts | 25,000 | 20,500 |
| Net realizable value | $205,000 | $205,000 |

As mentioned earlier, the allowance account can sometimes end up in a debit balance position after the write-off of an uncollectible account. This can happen if the write-offs in the period are more than the opening balance. It means the actual credit losses were greater than the estimated credit losses. The balance in Allowance for Doubtful Accounts will be corrected when the adjusting entry for estimated uncollectible accounts is made at the end of the period.

## 3. Recovery of an Uncollectible Account

Occasionally, a company collects cash from a customer after the account has been written off. Two entries are required to record the recovery of a bad debt: (1) The entry made in writing off the account is reversed to restore the customer's account. (2) The collection is recorded in the usual way.

To illustrate, assume that on July 1, 2008, Kids Online pays the $4,500 amount that had been written off on March 1. The entries are as follows:

| | (1) | | |
|---|---|---|---|
| July 1 | Accounts Receivable—Kids Online | 4,500 | |
| | Allowance for Doubtful Accounts | | 4,500 |
| | To reverse write-off of Kids Online account. | | |
| | (2) | | |
| July 1 | Cash | 4,500 | |
| | Accounts Receivable—Kids Online | | 4,500 |
| | To record collection from Kids Online. | | |

| A | = | L | + | OE |
|---|---|---|---|---|
| +4,500 | | | | |
| −4,500 | | | | |

Cash flows: no effect

| A | = | L | + | OE |
|---|---|---|---|---|
| +4,500 | | | | |
| −4,500 | | | | |

↑ Cash flows: +4,500

Note that the recovery of a bad debt, like the write-off of a bad debt, affects only balance sheet accounts. The net effect of the two entries is a debit to Cash and a credit to Allowance for Doubtful Accounts for $4,500. Accounts Receivable is debited and later credited for two reasons. First, the company must reverse the write-off. Second, Kids Online did pay, so the accounts receivable account in the general ledger and Kids Online's account in the subsidiary ledger, if a subsidiary ledger is used, should show this payment as it will need to be considered for deciding what credit to give to Kids Online in the future.

## Summary of Allowance Method

In summary, there are three types of transactions that you may need to record when valuing accounts receivable using the allowance method:

1. Estimates of uncollectible accounts receivable are recorded as adjusting entries at the end of the period by debiting Bad Debts Expense and crediting Allowance for Doubtful Accounts. The amount to record can be calculated using either the percentage of sales approach or the percentage of receivables approach.
2. Write-offs of actual uncollectible accounts are recorded in the next accounting period by debiting Allowance for Doubtful Accounts and crediting Accounts Receivable.

3. Later recoveries, if any, are recorded in two separate entries. The first reverses the write-off by debiting Accounts Receivable and crediting Allowance for Doubtful Accounts. The second records the normal collection of the account by debiting Cash and crediting Accounts Receivable.

These entries are summarized in the following T accounts:

| Accounts Receivable | | Allowance for Doubtful Accounts | |
|---|---|---|---|
| Beginning balance | Cash collections | Write-offs | Beginning balance |
| Credit sales | Write-offs | | Later recoveries |
| Later recoveries | | | Bad debt adjusting entry |
| Ending balance | | | Ending balance |

## BEFORE YOU GO ON . . .

### ▶Review It

1. How does the allowance method respect the matching principle?
2. Explain the differences between the percentage of sales and the percentage of receivables approaches.
3. How do write-offs and subsequent recoveries affect net income and the net realizable value of the accounts receivable when they are recorded?

### ▶Do It

The unadjusted trial balance at December 31 for Woo Wholesalers Co. shows the following selected information:

| | Debit | Credit |
|---|---|---|
| Accounts receivable | $120,000 | |
| Allowance for doubtful accounts | | $ 2,000 |
| Net credit sales | | 820,000 |

(a) Prepare the adjusting journal entry to record bad debts expense for each of the following *independent* situations:
1. Using the percentage of sales approach, Woo estimates uncollectible accounts to be 1% of net credit sales.
2. Using the percentage of receivables approach, Woo estimates uncollectible accounts to be as follows: 0–30 days, $85,000, 5% uncollectible; 31–60 days, $25,000, 15% uncollectible; and over 60 days, $10,000, 25% uncollectible.

(b) Calculate the net realizable value of Woo's accounts receivable for each of the above situations.

### Action Plan

- Percentage of sales: Apply the percentage to net credit sales to determine estimated bad debts expense—the adjusting entry amount. Ignore the balance in the allowance for doubtful accounts.
- Percentage of receivables: Apply percentages to the receivables in each age category to determine total estimated uncollectible accounts. The total amount determined in the aging schedule is the ending balance required in the allowance account, not the amount of the adjustment. Use the existing balance in the allowance account to determine the required adjusting entry.
- Net realizable value is equal to the balance in Accounts Receivable minus the balance in Allowance for Doubtful Accounts after the journal entry to record bad debts expense has been recorded.

## Solution

(a) 1.  Bad Debts Expense ($820,000 × 1%)    *IS approach*    8,200
            Allowance for Doubtful Accounts    8,200
                To record estimate of uncollectible accounts.

    2.  Bad Debts Expense ($10,500[1] − $2,000)    8,500
            Allowance for Doubtful Accounts    8,500
                To record estimate of uncollectible accounts.    *BS approach*
            [1] ($85,000 × 5%) + ($25,000 × 15%) + ($10,000 × 25%) = $10,500

(b) 1.  Net Realizable Value = Accounts Receivable − Allowance for Doubtful Accounts
                            = [$120,000 − ($2,000 + $8,200)]
                            = $109,800

    2.  Net Realizable Value = Accounts Receivable − Allowance for Doubtful Accounts
                            = [$120,000 − ($2,000 + $8,500)]
                            = $109,500

*Related exercise material:*   BE8–5, BE8–6, BE8–7, BE8–8, BE8–9, E8–4, E8–5, and E8–6.

# Notes Receivable

Credit may also be granted in exchange for a formal credit instrument known as a promissory note. A **promissory note** is a written promise to pay a specified amount of money on demand or at a definite time. Promissory notes may be used (1) when individuals and companies lend or borrow money, (2) when the amount of the transaction and the credit period are longer than normal limits, or (3) in settlement of accounts receivable.

study objective 3

Account for notes receivable.

In a promissory note, the party making the promise to pay is called the maker. For the maker of the promissory note, this is a note payable. The party to whom payment is to be made is called the payee. The payee may be specifically identified by name, or may be designated simply as the bearer of the note. For the payee of the promissory note, this is a note receivable.

The promissory note gives these details: the names of the parties, the amount of the loan, the loan period, the interest rate, and whether interest is repayable monthly or at maturity (the note's due date) along with the principal. Other details might include whether any security is pledged as collateral for the loan and what happens if the maker defaults (does not pay).

Students often find it difficult to understand the difference between a note receivable and an account receivable. An account receivable is an informal promise to pay, while a note receivable is a written promise to pay, which gives the payee a stronger legal claim. In addition, a note is a negotiable instrument (similar to a cheque), which means it can be transferred to another party by endorsement (signature of the payee). An account receivable results from a credit sale, while a note receivable can result from financing a purchase, lending money, or extending an account receivable beyond normal amounts or due dates. An account receivable is usually due in a short period of time (e.g., 30 days), while a note can extend for longer periods of time (e.g., 30 days to many years). An account receivable does not incur interest unless the account is overdue. A note usually bears interest for the entire period.

There are also similarities between notes and accounts receivable. Both are credit instruments. Both are valued at their net realizable values. Both can be sold to another party. The basic issues in accounting for notes receivable are the same as those for accounts receivable, as follows:

1. Recognizing notes receivable
2. Disposing of notes receivable

## Recognizing Notes Receivable

To illustrate the basic entry for notes receivable, we will assume that on May 31, Wolder Company (the payee) accepts a $10,000 note receivable from Higly Inc. (the maker), in settlement of an account receivable. The note has an annual interest rate of 6 percent and is due in four months, on September 30, at which time interest is also due.

The entry for the receipt of the note by Wolder Company is as follows:

| A | = | L | + | OE | | | |
|---|---|---|---|----|---|---|---|
| +10,000 | | | | | May 31 | Notes Receivable—Higly | 10,000 |
| −10,000 | | | | | |    Accounts Receivable—Higly |    10,000 |
| Cash flows: no effect | | | | | |    To record acceptance of Higly note. | |

If a note is exchanged for cash instead of an account receivable, the entry is a debit to Notes Receivable and a credit to Cash for the amount of the loan.

The note receivable is recorded at its principal value (the value shown on the face of the note). No interest revenue is reported when the note is accepted because, according to the revenue recognition principle, revenue is not recognized until it is earned. Interest is earned (accrued) as time passes.

## Recording Interest

As we learned in Chapter 3, the basic formula for calculating interest on an interest-bearing note is the following:

**Illustration 8-6 ▶**

Formula for calculating interest

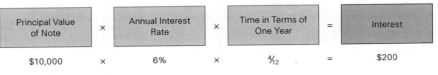

| Principal Value of Note | × | Annual Interest Rate | × | Time in Terms of One Year | = | Interest |
|---|---|---|---|---|---|---|
| $10,000 | × | 6% | × | $\frac{4}{12}$ | = | $200 |

The interest rate specified in a note is an annual rate of interest. The time factor in the above formula gives the fraction of the year that the note has been outstanding. As we did in past chapters, to keep it simple we will assume that interest is calculated in months rather than days. Illustration 8-6 shows the calculation of interest revenue for Wolder Company and interest expense for Higly Inc. for the term of the note.

If Wolder Company's year end was June 30, the following adjusting journal entry would be required to accrue interest for the month of June:

| A | = | L | + | OE | | | |
|---|---|---|---|----|---|---|---|
| +50 | | | | +50 | June 30 | Interest Receivable | 50 |
| Cash flows: no effect | | | | | |    Interest Revenue ($10,000 × 6% × $\frac{1}{12}$) |    50 |
| | | | | | |    To accrue interest on Higly note receivable. | |

Notice that interest on a note receivable is not debited to the Notes Receivable account. Instead, a separate account for the interest receivable is used. Since the note is a formal credit instrument, its recorded value stays the same as its face value.

## Valuing Notes Receivable

Like accounts receivable, notes receivable are reported at their net realizable value. Each note must be analyzed to determine how likely it is to be collected. If eventual collection is doubtful, bad debts expense and an allowance for doubtful notes must be recorded in the same way as is recorded for accounts receivable. Some companies use only one allowance account for both accounts and notes, and call it Allowance for Doubtful Accounts.

## Disposing of Notes Receivable

Notes are normally held to their maturity date, at which time the principal plus any unpaid interest is collected. This is known as honouring (paying) the note. Sometimes, the maker of the note defaults and an adjustment to the accounts must be made. This is known as dishonouring (not paying) the note.

### Honouring of Notes Receivable

A note is honoured when it is paid in full at its maturity date. The amount due at maturity is the principal of the note plus interest for the length of time the note is outstanding (assuming interest is due at maturity rather than monthly). If Higly Inc. honours the note when it is due on September 30, the maturity date, the entry by Wolder Company to record the collection is:

| Sept. 30 | Cash | 10,200 | |
| | Notes Receivable—Higly | | 10,000 |
| | Interest Revenue | | 150 |
| | Interest Receivable | | 50 |
| | To record collection of Higly note. | | |

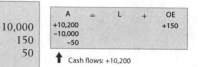

Recall that one month of interest revenue, $50 ($10,000 × 6% × $\frac{1}{12}$), was accrued on June 30, Wolder's year end. Consequently, only three months of interest revenue, $150 ($10,000 × 6% × $\frac{3}{12}$), is recorded in this period.

### Dishonouring of Notes Receivable

A **dishonoured note** is a note that is not paid in full at maturity. Since a dishonoured note receivable is no longer negotiable, the Notes Receivable account must be reduced by the principal of the note. The payee still has a claim against the maker of the note for both the principal and any unpaid interest and will transfer the amount owing to an Accounts Receivable account if there is hope that the amount will eventually be collected.

To illustrate, assume that on September 30 Higly Inc. says that it cannot pay at the present time but Wolder Company expects eventual collection. Wolder would make the following entry at the time the note is dishonoured:

| Sept. 30 | Accounts Receivable—Higly | 10,200 | |
| | Notes Receivable—Higly | | 10,000 |
| | Interest Revenue | | 150 |
| | Interest Receivable | | 50 |
| | To record dishonouring of Higly note where collection is expected. | | |

| A | = | L | + | OE |
|---|---|---|---|---|
| +10,200 | | | | +150 |
| −10,000 | | | | |
| −50 | | | | |

Cash flows: no effect

Wolder will continue to follow up with Higly. If the amount owing is eventually collected, Wolder will simply debit Cash and credit Accounts Receivable. If Wolder decides at a later date that it will never collect this amount from Higly, Wolder will write off the account receivable in the same way we learned earlier in the chapter—debit Allowance for Doubtful Accounts, and credit Accounts Receivable.

On the other hand, Wolder could directly write the note off on September 30 if it decided there was no hope of collection. Assuming Wolder uses one allowance account for both accounts and notes, it would record the following:

| A | = | L | + | OE |
|---|---|---|---|---|
| +10,050 | | | | |
| −10,000 | | | | |
| −50 | | | | |

Cash flows: no effect

| Sept. 30 | Allowance for Doubtful Accounts | 10,050 | |
|---|---|---|---|
| |     Notes Receivable—Higly | | 10,000 |
| |     Interest Receivable | | 50 |
| |         To record dishonouring of Higly note where collection is not | | |
| |         expected. | | |

No interest revenue is recorded, because collection will not occur. The interest receivable that previously had been accrued is also written off.

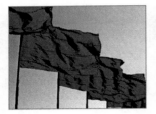

### ACCOUNTING IN ACTION ▶ Across the Organization Insight

Is China at risk of a massive financial crisis? According to the accounting firm Ernst & Young, uncollectible notes—called non-performing loans—in the Chinese financial system have reached a staggering U.S. $911 billion. What has caused this level of bad loans?

Politics is being blamed. The Communist party is relying on the lending practices of the state-controlled banks to ensure the survival of a one-party state. As ideological indoctrination can no longer be used to keep its members' loyalty, the Communist party is instead using political patronage. To keep them happy, party officials are appointed to executive positions in state-owned enterprises, where they are expected to prove that they are competent managers. This then requires the party to give these state-owned enterprises access to capital, mainly bank loans, even if an enterprise undertakes projects that are unlikely to succeed.

As a result, it is not surprising that the Chinese central bank reported that politically directed lending is the reason for most of its non-performing loans.

*Source:* Minxin Pei, "Politics Blamed for China's Trillion-Dollar Bad Debts," *The Australian*, May 9, 2006.

**?** If you were a loans officer at a bank, how would you decide whether or not to make a loan to a company?

### BEFORE YOU GO ON . . .

▶**Review It**

1. Explain the differences between an account receivable and a note receivable.
2. How is interest calculated for a note receivable?
3. At what value are notes receivable reported on the balance sheet?
4. Explain the difference between honouring and dishonouring a note receivable.

▶**Do It**

On May 1, Gambit Stores accepts from J. Nyznyk a $3,400, 3-month, 5% note in settlement of Nyznyk's overdue account. Interest is due at maturity. Gambit has a June 30 year end. (a) What are the entries made by Gambit on May 1, June 30, and on the maturity date August 1, assuming Nyznyk pays the note at that time? (b) What is the entry on August 1 if Nyznyk does not pay the note and collection is not expected in the future?

**Action Plan**

- Calculate the accrued interest. The formula is: Face value × annual interest rate × time in terms of one year.
- Record the interest accrued on June 30 to correctly apply the revenue recognition principle. Use Interest Receivable not Notes Receivable for accrued interest.
- If the note is honoured, calculate the interest accrued after June 30 and the total interest on the note. Record the interest accrued and the collection of the note and the total interest.
- If the note is dishonoured, record the transfer of the note and any interest earned to an accounts receivable account if eventual collection is expected or to an allowance account if collection is not expected.

## Solution

(a)

| | | | | |
|---|---|---|---:|---:|
| May 1 | Notes Receivable—J. Nyznyk | | 3,400 | |
| | Accounts Receivable—J. Nyznyk | | | 3,400 |
| | | To replace account receivable with 5% note receivable, due August 1. | | |
| Jun. 30 | Interest Receivable | | 28 | |
| | Interest Revenue ($3,400 \times 5\% \times \frac{2}{12}$) | | | 28 |
| | | To record interest earned to June 30. | | |
| Aug. 1 | Cash | | 3,442 | |
| | Interest Receivable | | | 28 |
| | Notes Receivable—J. Nyznyk | | | 3,400 |
| | Interest Revenue ($3,400 \times 5\% \times \frac{1}{12}$) | | | 14 |
| | | To record collection of Nyznyk note plus interest. | | |

(b)

| | | | | |
|---|---|---|---:|---:|
| Aug. 1 | Allowance for Doubtful Accounts | | 3,414 | |
| | Interest Receivable | | | 14 |
| | Notes Receivable—J. Nyznyk | | | 3,400 |
| | | To record dishonouring of Nyznyk note as collection is not expected. | | |

*Related exercise material:* BE8–10, BE8–11, BE8–12, E8–7, and E8–8.

# Statement Presentation and Management of Receivables

The way receivables are presented in the financial statements is important because receivables are directly affected by how a company recognizes its revenue and bad debts expense. In addition, these reported numbers are critical for analyzing the liquidity of a company and how well a company manages its receivables. In the next sections, we will discuss the presentation, analysis, and management of receivables.

study objective 4

Demonstrate the presentation, analysis, and management of receivables.

## Presentation

Each of the major types of receivables should be identified in the balance sheet or in the notes to the financial statements. Short-term receivables are reported in the current assets section of the balance sheet, following cash and short-term investments. Although only the net amount of receivables must be disclosed, it is helpful to report both the gross amount of receivables and the allowance for doubtful accounts either in the statement or in the notes to the financial statements. Notes receivable are often listed before accounts receivable because notes are more easily converted to cash.

On the following page the current assets presentation of receivables for Research in Motion Limited is shown:

| RESEARCH IN MOTION LIMITED<br>Balance Sheet (partial)<br>March 4, 2006<br>(in U.S. thousands) | |
| --- | --- |
| **Current assets** | |
| Cash and cash equivalents | $  459,540 |
| Short-term investments | 175,553 |
| Trade receivables | 315,278 |
| Other receivables | 31,861 |
| Inventory | 134,523 |
| Other current assets | 45,035 |
| Deferred income tax asset | 94,789 |
| | $1,256,579 |

In Note 1 to its financial statements, Research in Motion (RIM) states that its trade receivables include invoiced and accrued revenue and are presented net of an allowance for doubtful accounts of $1,551 thousand. The company also tells us that the allowance for doubtful accounts reflects estimates of probable losses in trade receivables. RIM explains that when it becomes aware of a specific customer's inability to meet its financial obligations, RIM records a specific bad debt provision to reduce the customer's related trade receivable to its estimated net realizable value. If the circumstances of specific customers change, RIM could then adjust its estimates of the recoverability of its trade receivables balances.

If a company has a significant risk of uncollectible accounts or other problems with receivables, it is required to disclose this possibility in the notes to the financial statements. RIM discloses that it depends on several significant customers and on large complex contracts with respect to sales of the majority of its products. RIM states that three customers account for 44 percent of its total trade receivables—one customer for 18 percent or almost $57 million. With trade receivables that large, it clearly makes good sense for RIM to closely monitor each account and calculate its allowance for doubtful accounts accordingly.

In the income statement, bad debts expense is reported in the operating expenses section. Interestingly, we are told in RIM's notes to the financial statements that it had a bad debt recovery (the opposite of an expense) of $552 thousand for the year ended March 4, 2006. This means RIM must have overestimated its bad debts expense in previous years and is now able to recover (reverse) these expenses. This shows just how difficult it can be to accurately estimate uncollectible accounts.

## Analysis

Managers need to carefully watch the relationship between sales, accounts receivable, and cash collections. If sales increase, then accounts receivable are also expected to increase. But an unusually high increase in accounts receivable might signal trouble. Perhaps the company increased its sales by loosening its credit policy, and these receivables may be difficult or impossible to collect. The company could also end up with higher costs because of the increase in sales since it may need more cash to pay for inventory and salaries.

Recall that the ability to pay obligations as they come due is measured by a company's liquidity. How can we tell if a company's management of its receivables is helping or hurting the company's liquidity? One way of doing this is to calculate a ratio called the **receivables turnover ratio**. This ratio measures the number of times, on average, that receivables are collected during the period. It is calculated by dividing net credit sales by average gross receivables during the year.

Unfortunately, companies rarely report the amount of net sales made on credit in their financial statements. As a result, net sales (including both cash and credit sales) is used as a substitute. In addition, because some companies do not publicly report their gross accounts receivable, net accounts receivable must be used. As long as the components that are used to calculate a ratio are the same for all companies being compared, however, the comparison is a fair one.

In Illustration 8-7, the substitute figures of total revenue and net accounts receivable were used to calculate the 2006 receivables turnover for Forzani (dollars in thousands).

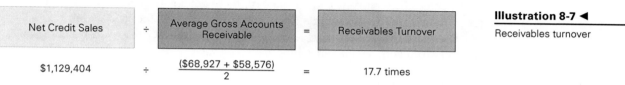

**Illustration 8-7 ◄**

Receivables turnover

The result indicates an accounts receivable turnover ratio of 17.7 times per year for Forzani. The higher the turnover ratio, the more liquid the company's receivables are.

A popular variation of the receivables turnover ratio is to convert it into the number of days it takes the company to collect its receivables. This ratio, called the **collection period**, is calculated by dividing 365 days by the receivables turnover, as shown for Forzani in Illustration 8-8.

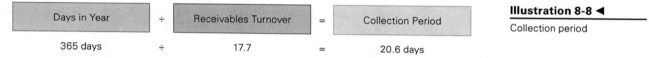

**Illustration 8-8 ◄**

Collection period

This means that in fiscal 2006 Forzani collected its receivables, on average, in approximately 20.6 days.

The collection period is often used to judge how effective a company's credit and collection policies are. The general rule is that the collection period should not be much longer than the credit term period (i.e., the time allowed for payment).

Both the receivables turnover and the collection period are useful for judging how efficiently a company converts its credit sales to cash. Remember that these measures should also be compared to industry averages, and to previous years.

In addition, these measures should also be analyzed along with other information about a company's liquidity, including the current ratio and inventory turnover. For example, low receivables may result in a low current ratio which might make the company look like it has poor liquidity. But the receivables may be low because they are turning over quickly. In general, the faster the turnover, the more reliable the current ratio is for assessing liquidity.

The collection period can also be used to assess the length of a company's operation cycle. Recall from Chapter 5 that the operating cycle is the average time that it takes to purchase inventory, sell it on account, and then collect cash from customers. In Chapter 6, we learned how to calculate days sales in inventory, which is the average age of the inventory on hand. The combination of the collection period and days sales in inventory is a useful way to measure the length of a company's operating cycle. Using the number of days to sell inventory calculated in Chapter 6, this calculation is shown in Illustration 8-9 for Forzani.

| Days to Sell Inventory | + | Collection Period | = | Operating Cycle in Days |
|---|---|---|---|---|
| 135 days | + | 20.6 days | = | 155.6 days |

**Illustration 8-9 ◄**

Operating cycle

This means that in fiscal 2006 it took 155.6 days on average from the time Forzani purchased its inventory until it collected cash.

## Accelerating Cash Receipts from Receivables

Normally, accounts receivable are collected in cash and removed from the books. However, as credit sales and receivables increase in size and significance, waiting for receivables to be collected causes increased costs from not being able to immediately use the cash that will be collected. If a company can collect cash more quickly from its receivables, it can shorten the cash-to-cash operating cycle discussed in the previous section.

There are two typical ways to collect cash more quickly from receivables: using the receivables to secure a loan and selling the receivables.

### Loans Secured by Receivables

One of the most common ways to speed up cash flow from accounts receivable is to go to a bank and borrow money using accounts receivable as collateral. While this does have a cost (interest has to be paid to the bank on the loan), the cash is available for the company to use earlier. The loan can then be repaid as the receivables are collected. Generally, banks are willing to give financing of up to 75 percent of receivables that are less than 90 days old. Quite often, these arrangements occur through an operating line of credit, which is discussed in a later chapter.

### Sale of Receivables

Companies also frequently sell their receivables to another company for cash. There are three reasons for the sale of receivables. The first is their size. To be competitive, sellers often give financing to purchasers of their goods to encourage the sale of the product. But the companies may not want to hold large amounts of receivables. As a result, many major companies in the automobile, truck, equipment, computer, and appliance industries have created wholly owned captive finance companies that accept responsibility for accounts receivable financing. An example is Ford Credit Canada, owned by Ford.

Second, receivables may be sold because they are the only reasonable source of cash. When money is tight, companies may not be able to borrow money in the usual credit markets. Even if credit is available, the cost of borrowing may be too high.

A final reason for selling receivables is that billing and collection are often time-consuming and costly. It is often easier for a retailer to sell its receivables to another party with expertise in billing and collection matters. Credit card companies, such as Visa and Master-Card, specialize in billing and collecting accounts receivable.

**Factoring.** One specific way to accelerate receivables collection is by sale to a factor. A **factor** is a finance company or bank which buys receivables from businesses and then collects the cash directly from the customer. If the customer does not pay, the business is usually responsible for reimbursing the factor for the uncollected amounts. This is known as selling receivables on a recourse basis.

**Securitization of Receivables.** An increasingly common way to accelerate receivables collection is to transfer receivables to investors in return for cash through a process called **securitization**. Receivables are sold to an independent trust which holds the receivables as an investment. This transforms the receivables into securities of the trust—which is why the term "securitization of receivables" is used. In some cases, the transfer is treated as a sale of receivables; in other cases, it is treated as a secured loan.

The differences between factoring and securitization are that securitization involves many investors and the cost is lower, the receivables are of higher quality, and the seller usually continues to be involved with collecting the receivables. In factoring, the sale is usually to only one company, the cost is higher, the receivables quality is lower, and the seller does not normally have any involvement with collecting the receivables.

For such companies as Canadian Pacific Railway, Canadian National Railway, and Petro-Canada, securitization of receivables appears to be an increasingly popular way of accelerating cash receipts from their receivables. Each of these companies reports details of the securitization of its receivables in the notes to its financial statements.

### ACCOUNTING IN ACTION ▶ Business Insight

On November 15, 2005, Sears Canada Inc. sold the assets and liabilities of its Credit and Financial Services operations, including its Sears Card and Sears MasterCard credit portfolio, to JPMorgan Chase & Co, a global financial services firm. Sears recorded income of $677.2 million on this sale. As part of the sale transaction, Sears and JPMorgan Chase entered into a long-term marketing and servicing alliance with an initial term of ten years. Under the alliance, Sears will receive performance payments from JPMorgan Chase based on a percentage of sales charged to the Sears Card and Sears MasterCard, new account generation, processing of account payments, and a percentage of sales of additional financial products by JPMorgan Chase to Sears Card and Sears MasterCard holders. In 2006, Sears expects that the alliance will generate annual performance payments of approximately $100 million. This amount is expected to partially replace the income previously reported in its Credit and Financial Services operations.

*Source:* Sears Canada Inc., 2005 Annual Report

**?** Why would Sears sell its credit card operations to an unrelated company?

---

## BEFORE YOU GO ON . . .

▶ **Review It**

1. Explain where and how accounts and notes receivable are reported on the balance sheet.
2. Where is bad debts expense reported on the income statement?
3. What do the receivables turnover and collection period reveal?
4. Why do companies want to accelerate cash receipts from receivables?

*Related exercise material:* BE8–13, BE8–14, BE8–15, E8–9, E8–10, E8–11, and E8–12.

# Demonstration Problem

Selected transactions for Dylan Co. follow. Dylan's year end is June 30.

Mar.  1  Sold $20,000 of merchandise to Potter Company, terms n/30.
      1  Accepted Juno Company's $16,500, 6-month, 6% note for the balance due on account.
     11  Potter Company returned $600 worth of goods.
     13  Made Dylan Co. credit card sales for $13,200.
     15  Made MasterCard credit sales that totalled $6,700. A 3% service fee is charged by MasterCard.
     30  Received payment in full from Potter Company.
Apr. 13  Received collections of $8,200 on Dylan Co. credit card sales. Added interest charges of 18% to the remaining balance.
May  10  Wrote off as uncollectible $15,000 of accounts receivable.
June 30  Dylan uses an aging schedule to estimate bad debts. Estimated uncollectible accounts are determined to be $20,000 at June 30. The allowance account has a $3,500 debit balance before the adjustment is recorded.
     30  Recorded the interest accrued on the Juno Company note.
July 16  One of the accounts receivable written off in May pays the amount due, $4,000, in full.
Sept. 1  Collected cash from Juno Company in payment of the March 1 note receivable.

## Instructions

Prepare the journal entries for the transactions. Dylan Co. uses a periodic inventory system.

## Action Plan

- Record accounts receivable at the invoice price.
- Recognize that sales returns and allowances reduce the amount received on accounts receivable.
- Recall that bank credit card sales are cash sales and company credit card sales are credit sales.
- Calculate interest by multiplying the interest rate by the face value by the part of the year that has passed.
- Record write-offs of accounts and recoveries of accounts written off only in balance sheet accounts.
- Consider any existing balance in the allowance account when making the adjustment for uncollectible accounts.
- Recognize any remaining interest on notes receivable when recording the collection of a note.

## Solution to Demonstration Problem

| | | | |
|---|---|---:|---:|
| Mar. 1 | Accounts Receivable—Potter | 20,000 | |
| | Sales | | 20,000 |
| | To record sale on account. | | |
| 1 | Notes Receivable—Juno | 16,500 | |
| | Accounts Receivable—Juno | | 16,500 |
| | To record acceptance of Juno Company note. | | |
| 11 | Sales Returns and Allowances | 600 | |
| | Accounts Receivable—Potter | | 600 |
| | To record return of goods. | | |
| 13 | Accounts Receivable | 13,200 | |
| | Sales | | 13,200 |
| | To record company credit card sales. | | |
| 15 | Cash | 6,499 | |
| | Credit Card Expense (3% × $6,700) | 201 | |
| | Sales | | 6,700 |
| | To record bank credit card sales. | | |
| 30 | Cash ($20,000 − $600) | 19,400 | |
| | Accounts Receivable—Potter | | 19,400 |
| | To record collection of accounts receivable. | | |
| Apr. 13 | Cash | 8,200 | |
| | Accounts Receivable | | 8,200 |
| | To record collection of credit card accounts receivable. | | |
| 13 | Accounts Receivable [($13,200 − $8,200) × 18% × $\frac{1}{12}$] | 75 | |
| | Interest Revenue | | 75 |
| | To record interest on amount due. | | |
| May 10 | Allowance for Doubtful Accounts | 15,000 | |
| | Accounts Receivable | | 15,000 |
| | To record write-off of accounts receivable. | | |

| | | | |
|---|---|---|---|
| June 30 | Bad Debts Expense ($20,000 + $3,500) | 23,500 | |
| | Allowance for Doubtful Accounts | | 23,500 |
| | To record estimate of uncollectible accounts. | | |
| 30 | Interest Receivable ($16,500 × 6% × $\frac{1}{12}$) | 330 | |
| | Interest Revenue | | 330 |
| | To record interest earned. | | |
| July 16 | Accounts Receivable | 4,000 | |
| | Allowance for Doubtful Accounts | | 4,000 |
| | To reverse write-off of accounts receivable. | | |
| 16 | Cash | 4,000 | |
| | Accounts Receivable | | 4,000 |
| | To record collection of accounts receivable. | | |
| Sept. 1 | Cash [$16,500 + ($16,500 × 6% × $\frac{6}{12}$)] | 16,995 | |
| | Interest Revenue ($16,500 × 6% × $\frac{2}{12}$) | | 165 |
| | Interest Receivable | | 330 |
| | Note Receivable | | 16,500 |
| | To record collection of note receivable plus interest. | | |

# Summary of Study Objectives

1. **Record accounts receivable transactions.** Accounts receivable are recorded at the invoice price. They are reduced by sales returns and allowances, and sales discounts. Accounts receivable subsidiary ledgers are used to keep track of individual account balances. When interest is charged on a past-due receivable, this interest is added to the accounts receivable balance and is recognized as interest revenue. Sales using non-bank credit cards result in a receivable, net of the credit card charges, from the credit card company; sales using company credit cards result in a receivable from the customer.

2. **Calculate the net realizable value of accounts receivable and account for bad debts.** The allowance method is used to match expected bad debts expense against sales revenue in the period when the sales occur. There are two approaches that can be used to estimate the bad debts: (1) percentage of sales, or (2) percentage of receivables. The percentage of sales approach emphasizes the matching principle. The percentage of receivables approach emphasizes the net realizable value of the accounts receivable. An aging schedule is usually used with the percentage of receivables approach. Uncollectible accounts are deducted from gross accounts receivable to report accounts receivable at their net realizable value in the balance sheet.

3. **Account for notes receivable.** Notes receivable are recorded at their principal, or face, value. Interest is earned from the date the note is issued until it matures and must be recorded in the correct accounting period. Interest receivable is recorded in a separate account from the note. Like accounts receivable, notes receivable are reported at their net realizable value.

Notes are normally held to maturity. At that time, the principal plus any unpaid interest is due and the note is removed from the accounts. If a note is not paid at maturity, it is said to be dishonoured. If eventual collection is still expected, an account receivable replaces the note receivable and any unpaid interest. Otherwise, the note must be written off.

4. **Demonstrate the presentation, analysis, and management of receivables.** Each major type of receivable should be identified in the balance sheet or in the notes to the financial statements. It is desirable to report the gross amount of receivables and the allowance for doubtful accounts/notes. Bad debts expense is reported in the income statement as an operating expense.

The liquidity of receivables can be evaluated by calculating the receivables turnover and collection period ratios. The receivables turnover is calculated by dividing net credit sales by average gross accounts receivable. This ratio measures how efficiently the company is converting its receivables into sales. The collection period converts the receivables turnover into days, dividing 365 days by the receivables turnover ratio. It shows the number of days, on average, it takes a company to collect its accounts receivable. The combination of the collection period and days sales in inventory is a useful way to measure the length of a company's operating cycle.

There are two typical ways to accelerate the receipt of cash from receivables: using the receivables to secure a loan and selling the receivables either to a factor or by securitizing them.

# Glossary

Study Aids: Glossary
Practice Tools: Key Term Matching Activity

**Accounts receivable**   Amounts owed by customers on account. (p. 408)

**Aging schedule**   A list of accounts receivable organized by the length of time they have been unpaid. (p. 416)

**Allowance method**   A method of accounting for bad debts that involves estimating uncollectible accounts at the end of each period. (p. 414)

**Bad debts expense**   An expense account to record uncollectible receivables. (p. 413)

**Balance sheet approach**   Another name for the percentage of receivables approach. (p. 417)

**Collection period**   The average number of days that receivables are outstanding. It is calculated by dividing 365 days by the receivables turnover. (p. 427)

**Dishonoured note**   A note that is not paid in full at maturity. (p. 423)

**Factor**   A finance company or bank that buys receivables from businesses and then collects the payments directly from the customers. (p. 428)

**Income statement approach**   Another name for the percentage of sales approach. (p. 416)

**Net realizable value**   Gross receivables less allowance for doubtful accounts. The net amount of receivables expected to be received in cash. (p. 412)

**Notes receivable**   Claims for which formal instruments of credit are issued as evidence of the debt. (p. 408)

**Percentage of receivables approach**   An approach to estimating uncollectible accounts where the allowance for doubtful accounts is calculated as a percentage of receivables. (p. 416)

**Percentage of sales approach**   An approach to estimating uncollectible accounts where bad debts expense is calculated as a percentage of net credit sales. (p. 415)

**Promissory note**   A written promise to pay a specified amount of money on demand or at a definite time. (p. 421)

**Receivables turnover ratio**   A measure of the liquidity of receivables, calculated by dividing net credit sales by average gross accounts receivable. (p. 426)

**Securitization**   The transfer of assets such as receivables to a company that issues securities as collateral for the receivables. (p. 428)

**Trade receivables**   Accounts and notes receivable that result from sales transactions. (p. 408)

# Self-Study Questions

Practice Tools: Self-Assessment Quizzes

Answers are at the end of the chapter.

(SO 1) AP   1. On June 15, Patel Company sells merchandise on account to Bullock Co. for $1,000, terms 2/10, n/30. On June 20, Bullock returns merchandise worth $300 to Patel. On June 24, payment is received from Bullock for the balance due. What is the amount of cash received?
(a) $680      (c) $700
(b) $686      (d) $980

(SO 2) AP   2. Sanderson Company has a credit balance of $5,000 in Allowance for Doubtful Accounts before any adjustments are made. Based on a review and aging of its accounts receivable at the end of the period, the company estimates that $60,000 of its receivables are uncollectible. The amount of bad debts expense which should be reported for this accounting period is:
(a) $5,000.      (c) $60,000.
(b) $55,000.      (d) $65,000.

3. Assume Sanderson Company has a debit balance of   (SO 2)
$5,000 in Allowance for Doubtful Accounts before any adjustments are made. Based on a review and aging of its accounts receivable at the end of the period, the company estimates that $60,000 of its receivables are uncollectible. The amount of bad debts expense which should be reported for this accounting period is:
(a) $5,000.      (c) $60,000
(b) $55,000.      (d) $65,000.

4. Net sales for the month are $800,000 and bad debts are   (SO 2)
expected to be 1.5% of net sales. The company uses the percentage of sales approach. If Allowance for Doubtful Accounts has a credit balance of $15,000 before adjustment, what is the balance in the allowance account after adjustment?
(a) $15,000      (c) $27,000
(b) $23,000      (d) $12,000

(SO 2) AP 5. On January 1, 2008, Allowance for Doubtful Accounts had a credit balance of $18,000. In 2008, $30,000 of uncollectible accounts receivable were written off. On December 31, 2008, the company had accounts receivable of $750,000. Past experience indicates that 3% of total receivables will become uncollectible. What should the adjusted balance of Allowance for Doubtful Accounts be at December 31, 2008?

(a) $4,500   (c) $22,500
(b) $10,500   (d) $40,500

(SO 3) AP 6. Sorenson Co. accepts a $1,000, 3-month, 8% promissory note in settlement of an account with Parton Co. The entry to record this transaction is:

| | | |
|---|---|---|
| (a) Notes Receivable | 1,020 | |
| Accounts Receivable | | 1,020 |
| (b) Notes Receivable | 1,000 | |
| Accounts Receivable | | 1,000 |
| (c) Notes Receivable | 1,000 | |
| Sales | | 1,000 |
| (d) Notes Receivable | 1,080 | |
| Accounts Receivable | | 1,080 |

(SO 3) AP 7. Schlicht Co. holds Osgrove Inc.'s $10,000, 4-month, 9% note. If no interest has been accrued when the note is collected, the entry made by Schlicht Co. is:

| | | |
|---|---|---|
| (a) Cash | 10,300 | |
| Notes Receivable | | 10,300 |
| (b) Cash | 10,900 | |
| Interest Revenue | | 900 |
| Notes Receivable | | 10,000 |
| (c) Accounts Receivable | 10,300 | |
| Notes Receivable | | 10,000 |
| Interest Revenue | | 300 |
| (d) Cash | 10,300 | |
| Notes Receivable | | 10,000 |
| Interest Revenue | | 300 |

(SO 4) K 8. Accounts and notes receivable are reported in the current assets section of the balance sheet at:
(a) net realizable value.
(b) net book value.
(c) lower of cost and market value.
(d) invoice cost.

(SO 4) AP 9. Moore Company had net credit sales of $800,000 in the year and a cost of goods sold of $500,000. The balance in Accounts Receivable at the beginning of the year was $100,000 and at the end of the year it was $150,000. What were the receivables turnover and collection period ratios, respectively?
(a) 4.0 and 91 days   (c) 6.4 and 57 days
(b) 5.3 and 69 days   (d) 8.0 and 46 days

(SO 4) K 10. Which of the following statements about securitization of accounts receivable is correct?
(a) Usually the seller continues to be involved with collection of the receivables.
(b) The receivables must be of high quality to qualify for securitization.
(c) Securitization of receivables is a relatively low-cost method of accelerating the receipt of cash.
(d) All of the above are correct.

the navigator

# Questions

(SO 1) K 1. Describe the three major types of receivables.

(SO 1) K 2. Why are accounts receivable and notes receivable sometimes called trade receivables?

(SO 1) C 3. (a) What are the advantages of using an accounts receivable subsidiary ledger? (b) Describe the relationship between the general ledger control account and the subsidiary ledger.

(SO 1) C 4. Ashley Dreher is confused about how a retail company should record a credit card sale. She thinks it does not matter if the customer used a bank credit card, a nonbank credit card, or a company credit card—the retail company should always debit Accounts Receivable because the customer is not paying in cash. Is Ashley correct? Explain.

(SO 2) C 5. Rod Ponach is the new credit manager for ACCT Company. He has told management there will be no bad debts in the future because he will do a complete credit check on each customer before the company makes a sale on

credit to the customer. Do you think Rod can completely eliminate bad debts for the company? Discuss.

(SO 2) K 6. Explain the allowance method of accounting for bad debts.

(SO 2) C 7. What is the purpose of the account Allowance for Doubtful Accounts? Although the normal balance of this account is a credit balance, it sometimes has a debit balance. Explain how this can happen.

(SO 2) C 8. Soo Eng cannot understand why net realizable value does not decrease when an uncollectible account is written off under the allowance method. Clarify this for Soo Eng.

(SO 2) C 9. Explain the difference between the two approaches that may be used in estimating uncollectible accounts under the allowance method.

(SO 2) K 10. Explain why the percentage of sales approach is also called the income statement approach and the percentage of receivables approach is also called the balance sheet approach.

(SO 2) K 11. Kyoto Company has a credit balance of $3,500 in Allowance for Doubtful Accounts. The estimated uncollectible amount under the percentage of sales approach is $4,100. The total estimated uncollectible amount under the percentage of receivables approach is $5,800. Describe the similarities and the differences in preparing the adjusting journal entry to record the estimated uncollectible accounts under each approach.

(SO 2) C 12. Why is the bad debts expense in the income statement typically not the same amount as the allowance for doubtful accounts amount in the balance sheet?

(SO 2) C 13. When an account receivable that was written off is later collected, two journal entries are usually made. Explain why.

(SO 3) K 14. Explain how notes receivable and accounts receivable are the same and how they are different.

(SO 3) C 15. Why might a company prefer to have a note receivable instead of an account receivable?

(SO 3) C 16. Why are notes receivable recorded at their principal value and not the amount that must be paid at maturity? Why is interest accrued on a note recorded in a separate account from the note receivable?

17. What does it mean if a note is dishonoured? What are the alternatives for the payee in accounting for a dishonoured note? (SO 3) C

18. Saucier Company has accounts receivable, notes receivable due in three months, notes receivable due in two years, an allowance for doubtful accounts, sales taxes recoverable, and income tax receivable. How should the receivables be reported on the balance sheet? (SO 4) C

19. The president proudly announces that her company's liquidity has improved. Its current ratio increased substantially this year. Does an increase in the current ratio always indicate improved liquidity? What other ratio(s) might you review to determine whether or not the increase in the current ratio is an improvement in the company's financial health? (SO 4) C

20. Does an increase in the receivables turnover indicate faster or slower collection of receivables? An increase or decrease in the collection period? (SO 4) C

21. Why do companies sometimes sell their receivables? (SO 4) K

22. As at December 31, 2005, **Canadian Pacific Railway Limited** had sold $120 million of its accounts receivable to an independent trust in a transaction known as securitization. Why might a company such as Canadian Pacific securitize its receivables? (SO 4) C

# Brief Exercises

Identify receivables.
(SO 1) K

**BE8–1**   Six transactions follow. Indicate the transactions that result in a receivable. For each transaction that does result in a receivable, would the receivable be reported as accounts receivable, notes receivable, or other receivables on a balance sheet?

(a) Advanced $10,000 to an employee.
(b) A customer pays $5,000 in advance for goods to be shipped the next month.
(c) Performed services for a customer in exchange for a $15,000 note.
(d) Sold merchandise on account to a customer for $60,000.
(e) Extended a customer's account for three months by accepting a note in exchange for it.
(f) Performed services for a customer who had paid in advance.

Record accounts receivable transactions.
(SO 1) AP

**BE8–2**   Record the following transactions on the books of Essex Co.:

(a) On July 1, Essex Co. sold merchandise on account to Cambridge Inc. for $14,000, terms 2/10, n/30. The cost of the merchandise sold was $9,000. Essex uses a perpetual inventory system.
(b) On July 3, Cambridge Inc. returned merchandise worth $2,400 to Essex Co. The original cost of the merchandise was $1,550. The merchandise was returned to inventory.
(c) On July 10, Cambridge Inc. paid for the merchandise.

Record accounts receivable transactions.
(SO 1) AP

**BE8–3**   Record the following transactions on the books of Lough Co.:

(a) On August 1, Lough Co. sold merchandise on account to Veale Inc. for $20,000, terms 2/10, n/30. Lough uses a periodic inventory system.
(b) On August 5, Veale Inc. returned merchandise worth $3,500 to Lough Co.

(c) On September 30, Lough Co. charged Veale Inc. one month's interest for the overdue account. Lough charges 21% on overdue accounts. (Round calculation to the nearest dollar.)

(d) On October 4, Veale Inc. paid the amount owing to Lough Co.

**BE8–4**   Stewart Department Store accepted a nonbank card in payment of a $200 purchase of merchandise on July 11. The credit card company charges a 3% fee. What entry should Stewart Department Store make? How would this entry change if the payment had been made with a Stewart Department Store credit card instead of a nonbank credit card? A Visa credit card instead of a nonbank credit card? Visa also charges a 3% fee.

*Record credit card transactions.*
*(SO 1) AP*

**BE8–5**   Qinshan Co. uses the percentage of sales approach to record bad debts expense. It estimates that 1.5% of net credit sales will become uncollectible. Credit sales are $900,000 for the year ended April 30, 2008; sales returns and allowances are $50,000; sales discounts are $10,000; and the allowance for doubtful accounts has a credit balance of $7,000. Prepare the adjusting entry to record bad debts expense in 2008.

*Record bad debts using percentage of sales approach.*
*(SO 2) AP*

**BE8–6**   Groleskey Co. uses the percentage of receivables approach to record bad debts expense. It estimates that 4% of total accounts receivable will become uncollectible. Accounts receivable are $500,000 at the end of the year. The allowance for doubtful accounts has a credit balance of $3,000.

*Record bad debts using percentage of receivables approach.*
*(SO 2) AP*

(a) Prepare the adjusting entry to record bad debts expense for the year ended December 31.
(b) If the allowance for doubtful accounts had a debit balance of $800 instead of a credit balance of $3,000, what amount would be reported for bad debts expense?

**BE8–7**   Refer to BE8–6. Groleskey Co. decides to refine its estimate of uncollectible accounts by preparing an aging schedule. Complete the following schedule and prepare the adjusting journal entry using this estimate. Assume Allowance for Doubtful Accounts has a credit balance of $3,000.

*Complete aging schedule and record bad debts expense.*
*(SO 2) AP*

| Number of Days Outstanding | Accounts Receivable | Estimated % Uncollectible | Estimated Uncollectible Accounts |
|---|---|---|---|
| 0–30 days | $315,000 | 1% | |
| 31–60 days | 90,000 | 4% | |
| 61–90 days | 60,000 | 10% | |
| Over 90 days | 35,000 | 20% | |
| Total | $500,000 | | |

**BE8–8**   At the end of 2007, Searcy Co. has an allowance for doubtful accounts of $54,000. On January 24, 2008, when it has accounts receivable of $680,000, Searcy Co. learns that an $18,000 receivable from Hutley Inc. is not collectible. Management authorizes a write-off.

*Record write-off and compare net realizable value.*
*(SO 2) AP*

(a) Record the write-off.
(b) What is the net realizable value of the accounts receivable (1) before the write-off, and (2) after the write-off?

**BE8–9**   Assume the same information as in BE8–8. Hutley's financial difficulties are over. On March 4, 2008, Searcy Co. receives an $18,000 payment in full from Hutley Inc. Record this transaction.

*Record recovery of account written-off.*
*(SO 2) AP*

**BE8–10**   Rocky Ridge Co. has three outstanding notes receivable at its December 31, 2007, fiscal year end. For each note calculate (a) total interest revenue, (b) interest revenue to be recorded in 2007, and (c) interest revenue to be recorded in 2008.

*Calculate interest accrued on notes receivable.*
*(SO 3) AP*

| Issue Date | Term | Principal | Interest Rate |
|---|---|---|---|
| 1. July 31, 2007 | 1 year | $16,000 | 7.50% |
| 2. September 1, 2007 | 6 months | 40,000 | 8.25% |
| 3. November 1, 2007 | 15 months | 39,000 | 6.75% |

Record notes receivable transactions.
(SO 3) AP

**BE8–11** On March 31, 2008, Raja Co. sold merchandise on account to Opal Co. for $12,000, terms n/30. Raja uses a perpetual inventory system and the merchandise had a cost of $7,500. On May 1, 2008, Opal gave Raja a 7%, 5-month promissory note in settlement of the account. Interest is to be paid at maturity. On October 1, Opal paid the note and accrued interest. Record the above transactions for Raja Co. Raja Co. has a June 30 fiscal year end and adjusts its accounts annually.

Record notes receivable transactions.
(SO 3) AP

**BE8–12** Lee Company accepts a $9,000, 3-month, 7% note receivable in settlement of an account receivable on April 1, 2008. Interest is to be paid at maturity. Lee Company has a December 31 year end and adjusts its accounts annually.

(a) Record (1) the issue of the note on April 1 and (2) the settlement of the note on July 1, assuming the note is honoured.
(b) Repeat part (a) assuming that the note is dishonoured but eventual collection is expected.
(c) Repeat part (a) assuming that the note is dishonoured and eventual collection is not expected.

Record notes receivable transactions and indicate statement presentation.
(SO 3, 4) AP

**BE8–13** Chant Co. lent Sharp Inc. $100,000 cash in exchange for a 5-year, 5% note on July 1, 2007. Interest is payable quarterly on January 1, April 1, July 1, and October 1 each year. Chant Co. has a December 31 year end. (a) Record Chant's entries related to the note to January 1, 2008. (b) What amounts related to this note will be reported on Chant's December 31, 2007, financial statements?

Prepare current assets section.
(SO 4) AP

**BE8–14** WAF Company's general ledger included the following accounts at November 30, 2008:

| | | | |
|---|---|---|---|
| Accounts payable | $124,200 | Interest receivable | $    995 |
| Accounts receivable | 95,000 | Inventory | 110,800 |
| Allowance for doubtful | | Note receivable— | |
|    accounts | 2,850 |    due April 23, 2009 | 20,000 |
| Bad debts expense | 3,730 | Note receivable— | |
| Cash | 34,000 |    due May 21, 2012 | 45,000 |
| GST recoverable | 1,990 | Prepaid expenses | 4,950 |

Prepare the current assets section of the balance sheet.

Calculate and interpret ratios.
(SO 4) AN

**BE8–15** The financial statements of **Maple Leaf Foods Inc.** report sales of $6,462,581 thousand for the year ended December 31, 2005. Accounts receivable are $247,014 thousand at the end of the year, and $292,462 thousand at the beginning of the year. Calculate Maple Leaf's receivables turnover and collection period. If the company's receivables turnover and collection period were 23.8 and 15.3 days, respectively, in the previous year, has the company's liquidity improved or weakened?

# Exercises

Record accounts receivable transactions.
(SO 1) AP

**E8–1** Links Costumes uses a perpetual inventory system. Selected transactions for April and June follow:

Apr.  6  Sold merchandise costing $3,200 to Pumphill Theatre for $6,500, terms 2/10, n/30.
      8  Pumphill returned $500 of the merchandise. This merchandise had originally cost Links $245 and was returned to inventory.
     16  Pumphill paid Links the amount owing.
     17  Sold merchandise costing $2,700 to EastCo Productions for $5,500, terms 2/10, n/30.
     18  EastCo returned $600 of the merchandise because it was damaged. The merchandise had originally cost Links $290. Links scrapped the merchandise.
June 17  Added interest charges for one month to the amount owning by EastCo. Links charges 21% on outstanding receivables.
     20  EastCo paid the amount owing.

**Instructions**

Record the above transactions.

**E8–2** Transactions follow for the Adventure Sports Co. store and three of its customers in the company's first month of business:

Mar. 2 Andrew Noren used his Adventure Sports credit card to purchase $570 of merchandise.
    4 Andrew returned $75 of merchandise for credit.
    5 Sold $380 of merchandise to Elaine Davidson, who used her Adventure Sports credit card.
    8 Erik Smistad purchased $421 of merchandise and paid for it in cash.
  17 Andrew Noren used his Adventure Sports credit card to purchase an additional $348 of merchandise.
  28 Erik Smistad used his Adventure Sports credit card to purchase $299 of merchandise.
  29 Elaine Davidson made a $100 payment on her credit card account.

*Record accounts receivable transactions. Post to subsidiary and general ledgers.*
*(SO 1) AP*

**Instructions**

(a) Record the above transactions. Adventure Sports uses a periodic inventory system.
(b) Set up general ledger accounts for the Accounts Receivable control account and for the Accounts Receivable subsidiary ledger accounts. Post the journal entries to these accounts.
(c) Prepare a list of customers and the balances of their accounts from the subsidiary ledger. Prove that the total of the subsidiary ledger is equal to the control account balance.

**E8–3** Kasko Stores accepts its own credit card, as well as bank and nonbank credit cards. In January and February, the following summary transactions occurred:

Jan. 5 Made $19,000 of Kasko credit card sales.
  20 Made $4,500 of Visa credit card sales (service charge fee, 3.25%).
  30 Made a $1,000 sale to a customer who used a nonbank credit card (service charge fee, 3.75%).
  31 Made debit card sales (service charge fee, $0.50 per transaction for 50 transactions) totalling $4,000.
Feb. 1 Collected $12,000 on Kasko credit card sales.
  14 Collected the amount owing from the credit card company for the January 30 transaction.
  28 Added interest charges of 24% to outstanding Kasko credit card balances.

*Record credit card transactions and indicate statement presentation.*
*(SO 1, 4) AP*

**Instructions**

(a) Record the above transactions for Kasko Stores.
(b) Where are interest revenue and credit card and debit card expenses reported in the income statement?

**E8–4** The ledger of Patillo Company at the end of the current year shows Accounts Receivable $90,000; Sales $970,000; Sales Returns and Allowances $40,000; and Sales Discounts $10,000.

*Record bad debts using two approaches.*
*(SO 2) AP*

**Instructions**

(a) If Allowance for Doubtful Accounts has a credit balance of $800 in the trial balance, record the adjusting entry at December 31, assuming bad debts are estimated to be (1) 1% of net sales, and (2) 10% of accounts receivable.
(b) If Allowance for Doubtful Accounts has a debit balance of $600 in the trial balance, record the adjusting entry at December 31, assuming bad debts are estimated to be (1) 0.5% of net sales, and (2) 5% of accounts receivable.

**E8–5** Grevina Company has accounts receivable of $92,500 at March 31. An analysis of the accounts shows the following:

*Prepare aging schedule and record bad debts.*
*(SO 2) AP*

| Month of Sale | Balance |
|---|---|
| March | $65,000 |
| February | 12,600 |
| January | 8,500 |
| October, November, and December | 6,400 |
| | $92,500 |

Credit terms are 2/10, n/30. At March 31, Allowance for Doubtful Accounts has a credit balance of $1,200 before adjustment. The company uses the percentage of receivables approach and an aging schedule to estimate uncollectible accounts. The company's percentage estimates of bad debts are as follows:

| Age of Accounts | Estimated % Uncollectible |
|---|---|
| 0–30 days outstanding | 2% |
| 31–60 days outstanding | 10% |
| 61–90 days outstanding | 25% |
| Over 90 days outstanding | 50% |

**Instructions**

(a) Prepare an aging schedule to determine the total estimated uncollectible accounts at March 31.

(b) Prepare the adjusting entry at March 31 to record bad debts expense.

(c) What are the advantages and disadvantages to Grevina Company of using an aging schedule to estimate uncollectible accounts, as compared to estimating uncollectible accounts as 10% of total accounts receivable?

Record bad debts, write-off, and recovery; calculate net realizable value.
(SO 2) AP

**E8–6** On December 31, 2007, when its Allowance for Doubtful Accounts had a debit balance of $1,000, Ceja Co. estimated that 2% of its $450,000 of accounts receivable would become uncollectible and recorded the bad debts adjusting entry. On May 11, 2008, when Ceja Co. had an Accounts Receivable balance of $471,000, the company determined that Robert Worthy's $1,850 account was uncollectible and wrote it off. On June 12, 2008, Worthy paid the amount previously written off.

**Instructions**

(a) Prepare the journal entries on December 31, 2007, May 11, 2008, and June 12, 2008.

(b) Post the journal entries to Allowance for Doubtful Accounts and calculate the new balance after each entry.

(c) Calculate the net realizable value of accounts receivable both before and after writing off Robert Worthy's account on May 11.

Record notes receivable transactions.
(SO 3) AP

**E8–7** Passera Supply Co. has the following transactions for notes receivable:

Nov. 1 Loaned $24,000 cash to A. Morgan on a 2-year, 8% note.

Dec. 1 Sold goods to Wright, Inc., receiving a $4,500, 3-month, 6% note. Passera uses the periodic method of accounting for inventory.

15 Received an $8,000, 6-month, 7% note on account from Barnes Company.

31 Accrued interest revenue on all notes receivable. Interest is due at maturity.

Mar. 1 Collected the amount owing on the Wright note.

**Instructions**

Record the transactions for Passera Supply Co. (Round calculations to the nearest dollar.)

Record notes receivable transactions.
(SO 3) AP

**E8–8** The following are notes receivable transactions for Prejear Co.:

Mar. 1 Received a $10,500, 9-month, 5% note on account from Jones Bros. Interest is due at maturity.

June 30 Accrued interest on the Jones note. June 30 is Prejear's year end and adjustments are recorded annually.

July 1 Lent $3,000 cash to Sarah Lough, receiving a 3-month, 6% note. Interest is due at maturity.

Oct. 1 Sarah Lough defaults on the note. Prejear does not expect to collect the amount owing in the future.

Dec. 1 Jones Bros. defaults on its note. Prejear expects to collect the amount owing in January.

**Instructions**

Record the transactions for Prejear Co. (Round calculations to the nearest dollar.)

Record notes receivable transactions and indicate statement presentation.
(SO 3, 4) AP

**E8–9** Ni Co. has the following notes receivable outstanding at December 31, 2008:

| | Issue Date | Term | Principal | Interest Rate |
|---|---|---|---|---|
| 1. | August 31, 2007 | 2 years | $15,000 | 4.50% |

| Issue Date | Term | Principal | Interest Rate |
|---|---|---|---|
| 2. October 1, 2007 | 18 months | 46,000 | 5.25% |
| 3. May 1, 2008 | 5 years | 22,000 | 5.75% |
| 4. October 31, 2008 | 7 months | 9,000 | 4.75% |

Interest is payable on the first day of each month for notes with terms of two years or longer. Interest is payable at maturity for notes with terms less than two years.

**Instructions**

(a) Calculate the interest revenue that Ni Co. will report on its income statement for the year ended December 31, 2008. Indicate where this will be presented on the income statement. (Round calculations to the nearest dollar.)

(b) Calculate the amounts related to these notes that will be reported on Ni Co.'s balance sheet at December 31, 2008. Indicate where they will be presented. Assume all required interest payments have been received on time. (Round calculations to the nearest dollar.)

**E8–10** In its first year of operations, AJS Company had sales of $3 million (all on credit) and cost of goods sold of $1,750,000. At year end, February 29, 2008, $600,000 of the sales remained uncollected. The credit manager estimates that $35,000 of these receivables will become uncollectible.

*Record bad debts, prepare partial balance sheet, and calculate ratios.*
*(SO 2, 4) AP*

(a) Prepare the journal entry to record the estimated uncollectibles.

(b) Prepare the current assets section of the balance sheet for AJS Company, assuming that in addition to the receivables it has the following: cash of $90,000; merchandise inventory of $365,000; accounts payable of $400,000; GST recoverable of $25,000; notes receivable of $45,000 due on April 22, 2008; and supplies of $10,000.

(c) Calculate the receivables turnover and collection period. (*Hint:* Remember that this is the end of the first year of business.)

**E8–11** The following information (in millions) was taken from the December 31 financial statements of **Canadian National Railway Company**:

*Calculate ratios.*
*(SO 4) AN*

| | 2005 | 2004 | 2003 |
|---|---|---|---|
| Accounts receivable, gross | $ 703 | $ 863 | $ 584 |
| Allowance for doubtful accounts | 80 | 70 | 55 |
| Accounts receivable, net | 623 | 793 | 529 |
| Revenues | 7,240 | 6,548 | 5,884 |
| Total current assets | 1,149 | 1,710 | 1,092 |
| Total current liabilities | 1,958 | 2,259 | 1,977 |

**Instructions**

(a) Calculate the 2005 and 2004 current ratios.
(b) Calculate the receivables turnover and average collection period for 2005 and 2004.
(c) Are accounts receivable a material component of the company's current assets?
(d) Comment on any improvement or weakening in CN's liquidity and its management of accounts receivable.

**E8–12** Refer to E8–11. In the notes to its financial statements, **Canadian National Railway Company** reports that it has a revolving agreement to sell eligible freight trade and other receivables up to a maximum of $500 million of receivables outstanding at any point in time. At December 31, 2005, the company had sold $489 million of these receivables, compared to $445 million at December 31, 2004. CN has retained the responsibility for servicing, administering, and collecting the freight receivables sold.

*Discuss sale of receivables.*
*(SO 4) C*

**Instructions**

Explain why CN, a financially stable company, securitizes (sells) such a large portion of its receivables.

# Problems: Set A

Record accounts receivable and bad debts transactions. (SO 1, 2) AP

**P8–1A** At December 31, 2007, Underwood Imports reported the following information on its balance sheet:

| | |
|---|---|
| Accounts receivable | $995,000 |
| Less: Allowance for doubtful accounts | 59,700 |

In 2008, the company had the following transactions related to receivables:

1. Sales on account, $2,620,000
2. Sales returns and allowances, $40,000
3. Collections of accounts receivable, $2,700,000
4. Write-offs of accounts deemed uncollectible, $75,000
5. Recovery of bad debts previously written off as uncollectible, $30,000

**Instructions**

(a) Prepare the summary journal entries to record each of these five transactions.
(b) Enter the January 1, 2008, balances in the Accounts Receivable and Allowance for Doubtful Accounts general ledger accounts. Post the entries to the two accounts and determine the balances at December 31, 2008.
(c) Record bad debts expense for 2008. Uncollectible accounts are estimated at 6% of accounts receivable.
(d) Calculate the net realizable value of accounts receivable at December 31, 2008.

Record accounts receivable and bad debts transactions. (SO 1, 2) AP

**P8–2A** At the beginning of the current period, Hong Co. had a balance of $300,000 in Accounts Receivable and an $18,000 credit balance in Allowance for Doubtful Accounts. In the period, it had sales on account of $1,950,000 and collections of $2,020,000. It wrote off accounts receivable of $29,500 as uncollectible. However, $3,500 of one of the accounts written off as uncollectible was recovered before the end of the current period.

**Instructions**

(a) Record sales and collections in the period.
(b) Record the write-off of uncollectible accounts and the recovery of accounts written off as uncollectible in the period.
(c) Determine the balance in Accounts Receivable and Allowance for Doubtful Accounts after recording the transactions in (a) and (b).
(d) Record the bad debts expense adjusting entry for the period if Hong Co. estimates that 6% of total accounts receivable will become uncollectible.
(e) What is the net realizable value of receivables at the end of the period?
(f) What is the bad debts expense on the income statement for the period? →
(g) Now assume that Hong Co. uses the percentage of sales approach instead of the percentage of receivables approach to estimate uncollectible accounts. Repeat (d) through (f) assuming Hong estimates 1.25% of the credit sales will become uncollectible.

Calculate bad debt amounts and answer questions. (SO 2) AP

**P8–3A** Information for Tisipai Company in 2008 follows:

| | |
|---|---|
| Total credit sales | $1,650,000 |
| Accounts receivable at December 31 | 625,000 |
| Accounts receivable written off | 24,000 |
| Accounts receivable later recovered | 4,000 |

**Instructions**

(a) If Tisipai Company does not use the allowance method, what amount will it report for bad debts expense?
(b) Assume instead that Tisipai Company uses the allowance method and estimates its bad debts expense to be 2.25% of credit sales. What amount of bad debts expense will the company record if Allowance for Doubtful Accounts has a credit balance of $3,500 before making the adjustment?

(c) Assume instead that Tisipai Company uses the allowance method and estimates its uncollectible accounts to be $42,000 based on an aging schedule. What amount of bad debts expense will the company record if Allowance for Doubtful Accounts has a credit balance of $3,500 before making the adjustment?

(d) Assume the same facts as in (c), except that there is a $2,250 debit balance in Allowance for Doubtful Accounts. What amount of bad debts expense will the company record?

(e) How does the write-off of an uncollectible account affect the net realizable value of accounts receivable?

(f) Why should companies use the allowance method of accounting for bad debts?

**P8–4A**  An aging analysis of Hake Company's accounts receivable at December 31, 2007 and 2008, showed the following:

*Prepare aging schedule and record bad debts.*
*(SO 2) AP*

| Number of Days Outstanding | Estimated % Uncollectible | December 31 2008 | 2007 |
|---|---|---|---|
| 0–30 days | 3% | $150,000 | $160,000 |
| 31–60 days | 6% | 32,000 | 57,000 |
| 61–90 days | 12% | 43,000 | 38,000 |
| Over 90 days | 24% | 65,000 | 25,000 |
| Total | | $290,000 | $280,000 |

Additional information:

1. At December 31, 2007, the unadjusted balance in Allowance for Doubtful Accounts was a credit of $4,500.
2. In 2008, $21,000 of accounts were written off as uncollectible and $1,500 of accounts previously written off were recovered.

**Instructions**

(a) Prepare an aging schedule to calculate the estimated uncollectible accounts at December 31, 2007, and at December 31, 2008. Comment on the results.

(b) Record the following transactions:
   1. The adjusting entry on December 31, 2007
   2. The write-off of uncollectible accounts in 2008
   3. The collection of accounts previously written off
   4. The adjusting entry on December 31, 2008

(c) Calculate the net realizable value of Hake's accounts receivable at December 31, 2007, and December 31, 2008.

**P8–5A**  Imagine Co. uses the allowance method to estimate uncollectible accounts receivable. The computer produced the following aging of the accounts receivable at year end:

*Prepare aging schedule and record bad debts.*
*(SO 2) AP*

| Customer | Total | Number of Days Outstanding | | | |
|---|---|---|---|---|---|
| | | 0–30 | 31–60 | 61–90 | 91–120 |
| Accounts receivable | $385,000 | $220,000 | $100,000 | $40,000 | $25,000 |
| Estimated % uncollectible | | 1% | 5% | 10% | 20% |
| Estimated uncollectible accounts | | | | | |

The unadjusted balance in Allowance for Doubtful Accounts is a debit of $10,000.

**Instructions**

(a) Complete the aging schedule and calculate the total estimated uncollectible accounts from the above information.

(b) Record the bad debts adjusting entry using the above information.

(c) In the following year, $17,800 of the outstanding accounts receivable is determined to be uncollectible. Record the write-off of the uncollectible accounts.

(d) The company collects $6,300 of the $17,800 of accounts receivable that were determined to be uncollectible in (c). No further amounts are expected to be collected. Prepare the journal entry (or entries) to record the recovery of this amount.

(e) Comment on how your answers to parts (a) to (d) would change if Imagine Co. used a percentage of total accounts receivable of 3% instead of aging the accounts receivable.

(f) What are the advantages for the company of aging the accounts receivable rather than applying a percentage to total accounts receivable?

**Determine missing amounts.**
**(SO 2) AN**

**P8–6A**  Armadillo and Company reported the following information in its general ledger at July 31:

| Accounts Receivable | | | | Sales | |
|---|---|---|---|---|---|
| Beg. bal. | 325,000 | | (b) | | (e) |
| | (a) | | (c) | | |
| End. bal. | 376,000 | | | | |

| Allowance for Doubtful Accounts | | | | Bad Debts Expense | |
|---|---|---|---|---|---|
| | | Beg. bal. | 22,750 | (f) | |
| | 21,550 | | (d) | | |
| | | End. bal. | 26,350 | | |

All sales were made on account. Bad debts expense was estimated as 1% of sales. There were no recoveries of accounts previously written off.

### Instructions

Determine the missing amounts in Armadillo and Company's accounts. State what each of these amounts represents. You will not be able to determine the missing items in alphabetical order. (*Hint:* To solve this problem, it might help if you reconstruct the journal entries.)

**Record accounts receivable and bad debts transactions; discuss statement presentation.**
**(SO 1, 2, 4) AP**

**P8–7A**  Assiniboia Co. uses the percentage of sales approach to record bad debts expense for its monthly financial statements and the percentage of receivables approach for its year-end financial statements. Assiniboia Co. has a May 31 fiscal year end, closes temporary accounts annually, and uses the periodic inventory system.

On March 31, 2008, after completing its month-end adjustments, it had accounts receivable of $892,500, a credit balance of $47,750 in Allowance for Doubtful Accounts, and a debit balance in Bad Debts Expense of $115,880. In April and May, the following occurred:

April
1. Sold $646,900 of merchandise on credit.
2. Accepted $10,900 of returns on the merchandise sold on credit. These customers were issued credit memos.
3. Collected $696,250 cash on account from customers.
4. Interest charges of $13,860 were charged to outstanding accounts receivable.
5. As part of the month-end adjusting entries, recorded bad debts expense of 3% of net credit sales for the month.

May
1. Credit sales were $763,600.
2. Received $4,450 cash from a customer whose account had been written off in March.
3. Collected $785,240 cash, in addition to the cash collected in (2) above, from customers on account.
4. Wrote off $69,580 of accounts receivable as uncollectible.
5. Interest charges of $12,070 were charged to outstanding accounts receivable.
6. Recorded the year-end adjustment for bad debts. Uncollectible accounts were estimated to be 6% of accounts receivable.

### Instructions

(a) Record the above transactions and adjustments.
(b) Show how accounts receivable will appear on the May 31, 2008, balance sheet.

(c) What amount will be reported as bad debts expense on the income statement for the year ended May 31, 2008?

(d) Where are bad debts expense and interest revenue shown on the income statement?

**P8–8A** On January 1, 2007, Vu Co. had accounts receivable of $146,000, notes receivable of $12,000, interest receivable of $100, and allowance for doubtful accounts of $13,200. The note receivable was a 5-month, 5% note receivable from Annabelle Company dated October 31, 2006; the correct interest has been accrued. Vu Co. prepares financial statements annually for the year ended December 31. Assume interest is due at maturity unless otherwise specified. In the year, the following selected transactions occurred:

*Record receivables transactions. (SO 2, 3) AP*

Jan.  2  Sold $16,000 of merchandise to George Company, terms 2/10, n/30.

Feb.  1  Accepted George Company's $16,000, 3-month, 6.5% note for the balance due (see January 2 transaction).

Mar. 31  Received payment in full from Annabelle Company for the amount due.

May   1  Collected George Company note in full (see February 1 transaction).

    25  Accepted Avery Inc.'s $6,000, 3-month, 6% note in settlement of a past-due balance on account. Interest is payable monthly.

June 25  Received one month's interest from Avery Inc. on its note (see May 25 transaction).

July 25  The Avery Inc. note was dishonoured (see May 25 transaction). Avery Inc. is bankrupt and future payment is not expected.

Sept. 1  Sold $10,000 of merchandise to Young Company and accepted a $10,000, 6-month, 5.25% note for the amount due.

Nov. 22  News reports indicate that several key officers of Young Company have been arrested on charges of fraud and embezzlement, and that the company's operations have been shut down indefinitely (see September 1 transaction).

    30  Gave MRC Corp a $5,000 cash loan and accepted MRC's 4-month, 4.5% note.

Dec. 31  Accrued interest is recorded on any outstanding notes at year end.

*Instructions*

(a) Record the above transactions.

(b) If there have been no further reports on the situation regarding Young Company, do you think the note should be written off? If not, do you think interest should be accrued on the note receivable at year end?

**P8–9A** Ouellette Co. adjusts its books monthly. On June 30, 2008, the general ledger includes the following account balances:

*Record receivable transactions. Show balance sheet presentation. (SO 1, 3, 4) AP*

| | |
|---|---|
| Notes Receivable | $29,800 |
| Credit Card Receivables | 11,500 |
| Interest Receivable | ? |

June 30, 08

Notes receivable include the following:

$6000 \times .06 \times \frac{1}{24} = 12$

| Issue Date | Maker | Principal | Term | Interest |
|---|---|---|---|---|
| May 1, 2007 | ALD Inc. | $ 6,000 | 2 years | 6.00% |
| October 31, 2007 | KAB Ltd. | 10,000 | 9 months | 5.50% |
| May 31, 2008 | DNR Co. | 4,800 | 2 months | 6.75% |
| June 30, 2008 | MJH Corp. | 9,000 | 18 months | 5.00% |

Interest is payable on the first day of each month for notes with terms of one year or longer. Interest is payable at maturity for notes with terms less than one year. In July, the following transactions were completed:

July   1  Received payment of the interest due from ALD Inc.

    5  Made sales of $7,800 on Ouellette credit cards.

   25  Collected $5,400 of Ouellette credit card receivables.

   31  Added $215 to Ouellette credit card customer balances for interest charges on unpaid balances.

July 31 Received notice that the DNR Co. note has been dishonoured. Assume that DNR Co. is expected to pay in the future.

**Instructions**

(a) Calculate the interest receivable at June 30, 2008.
(b) Record the July transactions and the July 31 adjusting entry for accrued interest receivable.
(c) Enter the balances at July 1 in the receivables accounts. Post the entries to all the receivables accounts.
(d) Show the balance sheet presentation of the receivables accounts at July 31, 2008.
(e) How would the journal entry on July 31 be different if DNR Co. were not expected to pay in the future?

*Prepare assets section of balance sheet; calculate and interpret ratios.*
*(SO 4) AN*

**P8–10A** Norlandia Saga Company's general ledger included the following selected accounts (in thousands) at November 30, 2008:

| | | | |
|---|---|---|---|
| Accounts payable | $ 682.7 | Interest revenue | $ 13.4 |
| Accounts receivable | 389.2 | Merchandise inventory | 420.6 |
| Accumulated amortization—equipment | 577.1 | Notes receivable—due in 2009 | 64.0 |
| Allowance for doubtful accounts | 18.5 | Notes receivable—due in 2012 | 127.4 |
| Bad debts expense | 54.5 | Prepaid expenses and deposits | 24.1 |
| Cash and cash equivalents | 802.2 | Sales | 3,529.7 |
| Cost of goods sold | 441.2 | Sales discounts | 23.1 |
| Equipment | 1,155.2 | Supplies | 19.9 |
| | | Unearned sales revenue | 50.3 |

Additional information:

1. The net realizable value of accounts receivable was $345.1 thousand on November 30, 2007.
2. The receivables turnover was 9.1 the previous year.

**Instructions**

(a) Prepare the assets section of the balance sheet.
(b) Calculate the receivables turnover and average collection period. Compare these results to the previous year's results and comment on any trends.

*Calculate and interpret ratios.*
*(SO 4) AN*

**P8–11A** Presented here is selected financial information (in U.S. millions) from the 2005 financial statements of **Nike** and **Adidas**:

| | Nike | Adidas |
|---|---|---|
| Sales | $13,739.7 | $6,635.6 |
| Allowance for doubtful accounts, Jan. 1 | 95.3 | 91.5 |
| Allowance for doubtful accounts, Dec. 31 | 80.4 | 80.7 |
| Accounts receivable balance (gross), Jan. 1 | 2215.5 | 1137.8 |
| Accounts receivable balance (gross), Dec. 31 | 2342.5 | 1045.5 |

**Instructions**

Calculate the receivables turnover and average collection period for both companies and compare the two companies. Comment on the difference in the two companies' collection experiences.

*Evaluate liquidity.*
*(SO 4) AN*

**P8–12A** The following ratios are available for Western Roofing:

| | 2008 | 2007 | 2006 |
|---|---|---|---|
| Current ratio | 1.6 to 1 | 1.5 to 1 | 1.4 to 1 |
| Receivables turnover | 6 times | 7 times | 8 times |
| Inventory turnover | 7 times | 6 times | 5 times |

**Instructions**

(a) Calculate the collection period, days sales in inventory, and operating cycle for each year.
(b) Has Western Roofing's liquidity improved or weakened over the three-year period? Explain.

# Problems: Set B

**P8–1B**  At December 31, 2007, Bordeaux Co. reported the following information on its balance sheet:

|  |  |
|---|---|
| Accounts receivable | $960,000 |
| Less: Allowance for doubtful accounts | 67,200 |

*Record accounts receivable and bad debts transactions.*
*(SO 1, 2) AP*

In the first quarter of 2008, the company had the following transactions related to receivables:

1. Sales on account, $3,200,000
2. Sales returns and allowances, $50,000
3. Collections of accounts receivable, $3,000,000
4. Write-offs of accounts considered uncollectible, $90,000
5. Recovery of accounts previously written off as uncollectible, $18,000

**Instructions**

(a) Prepare the summary journal entries to record each of these five transactions.
(b) Enter the January 1, 2008, balances in the Accounts Receivable and Allowance for Doubtful Accounts general ledger accounts. Post the entries to the two accounts and determine the balances.
(c) Record bad debts expense for the first quarter of 2008. Uncollectible accounts are estimated at 7% of accounts receivable.
(d) Calculate the net realizable value of accounts receivable at the end of the first quarter.

**P8–2B**  At the beginning of the current period, Huang Co. had a balance of $200,000 in Accounts Receivable and a $16,000 credit balance in Allowance for Doubtful Accounts. In the period, it had net credit sales of $800,000 and collections of $723,000. It wrote off accounts receivable of $21,750 as uncollectible. However, $3,300 of one of the accounts written off as uncollectible was recovered before the end of the current period.

*Record accounts receivable and bad debts transactions.*
*(SO 1, 2) AP*

**Instructions**

(a) Record sales and collections in the period.
(b) Record the write-off of uncollectible accounts and the recovery of accounts written off as uncollectible in the period.
(c) Record the bad debts expense adjusting entry for the period if Huang Co. estimates that 2.25% of net credit sales will become uncollectible.
(d) Determine the ending balances in Accounts Receivable and Allowance for Doubtful Accounts.
(e) What is the net realizable value of receivables at the end of the period?
(f) What is the amount of bad debts expense on the income statement for the period?
(g) Now assume that Huang Co. uses the percentage of receivables approach instead of the percentage of sales approach to estimate uncollectible accounts. Repeat (c) through (f) assuming Huang estimates 8% of the ending accounts receivable will become uncollectible.

**P8–3B**  Information on Hohenberger Company for 2008 follows:

|  |  |
|---|---|
| Total credit sales | $2,000,000 |
| Accounts receivable at December 31 | 800,000 |
| Uncollectible accounts written off | 35,000 |
| Uncollectible accounts later recovered | 6,000 |

*Calculate bad debt amounts and answer questions.*
*(SO 2) AP*

**Instructions**

(a) If Hohenberger Company does not use the allowance method, what amount will it report for bad debts expense?
(b) Assume instead that Hohenberger Company uses the allowance method and estimates its bad debts expense at 2.5% of credit sales. What amount of bad debts expense will Hohenberger Company record if Allowance for Doubtful Accounts has a credit balance of $4,000 before making the adjustment?

(c) Assume instead that Hohenberger Company estimates its bad debts expense based on 6% of total accounts receivable. What amount of bad debts expense will Hohenberger Company record if it has an Allowance for Doubtful Accounts credit balance of $4,000 before making the adjustment?

(d) Assume the same facts as in (c) except that there is a $3,000 debit balance in Allowance for Doubtful Accounts. What amount of bad debts expense will Hohenberger record?

(e) How does the write-off of an uncollectible account affect the bad debts expense for the current period?

(f) How does the collection of an account that had previously been written off affect the net realizable value of accounts receivable?

**Prepare aging schedule and record bad debts.**
(SO 2) AP

**P8–4B** An aging analysis of Hagiwara Company's accounts receivable at December 31, 2007 and 2008, showed the following:

| Number of Days Outstanding | Estimated % Uncollectible | December 31 2008 | 2007 |
|---|---|---|---|
| 0–30 days | 1.5% | $120,000 | $137,000 |
| 31–60 days | 6.0% | 32,000 | 61,000 |
| 61–90 days | 18.0% | 45,000 | 38,000 |
| Over 90 days | 40.0% | 78,000 | 24,000 |
| Total | | $275,000 | $260,000 |

Additional information:

1. At December 31, 2007, the unadjusted balance in Allowance for Doubtful Accounts was a credit of $5,700.
2. In 2008, $26,000 of accounts were written off as uncollectible and $1,200 of accounts previously written off were recovered.

**Instructions**

(a) Prepare an aging schedule to calculate the estimated uncollectible accounts at December 31, 2007, and at December 31, 2008. Comment on the results.

(b) Record the following transactions:
1. The adjusting entry on December 31, 2007
2. The write off of uncollectible accounts in 2008
3. The collection of accounts previously written off
4. The adjusting entry on December 31, 2008

(c) Calculate the net realizable value of Hagiwara's accounts receivable at December 31, 2007, and December 31, 2008.

**Prepare aging schedule and record bad debts.**
(SO 2) AP

**P8–5B** The following is selected information taken from a company's aging schedule to estimate uncollectible accounts receivable at year end:

| Customer | Total | Number of Days Outstanding 0–30 | 31–60 | 61–90 | 91–120 |
|---|---|---|---|---|---|
| Accounts receivable | $560,000 | $220,000 | $160,000 | $100,000 | $80,000 |
| Estimated % uncollectible | | 1% | 5% | 10% | 20% |
| Estimated uncollectible accounts | | | | | |

The unadjusted balance in Allowance for Doubtful Accounts is a credit of $7,000.

**Instructions**

(a) Complete the aging schedule and calculate the total estimated uncollectible accounts.

(b) Record the bad debts adjusting entry using the above information.

(c) In the following year, $32,000 of the outstanding accounts receivable is determined to be uncollectible. Record the write-off of the uncollectible accounts.

(d) The company collects $8,500 of the $32,000 of accounts that were determined to be uncollectible in (c). The company also expects to collect an additional $500. Record the journal entry (or entries) to restore the accounts receivable and the cash collected. Collection of the $500 is expected in the near future.

(e) Explain how establishing an allowance satisfies the matching principle.

**P8–6B** Kadakus and Company reported the following information in its general ledger at August 31:

*Determine missing amounts.*
*(SO 2) AN*

| Accounts Receivable | | | | Sales | |
|---|---|---|---|---|---|
| Beg. bal. | 845,000 | (b) | | | (f) |
| | (a) | (c) | | | |
| End. bal. | 927,500 | | | | |

| Allowance for Doubtful Accounts | | | | Bad Debts Expense | |
|---|---|---|---|---|---|
| | | Beg. bal. | 72,500 | 45,500 | |
| | (d) | (e) | | | |
| | | End. bal. | 79,600 | | |

All sales were made on account. Bad debts expense was estimated as 1% of sales. There were no recoveries of accounts previously written off.

### Instructions

Determine the missing amounts in Kadakus and Company's accounts. State what each of these amounts represents. You will not be able to determine the missing items in alphabetical order. (*Hint:* To solve this problem, it might help if you reconstruct the journal entries.)

**P8–7B** Bassano Company uses the percentage of sales approach to record bad debts expense for its monthly financial statements and the percentage of receivables approach for its year-end financial statements. Bassano Company has an October 31 fiscal year end, closes temporary accounts annually, and uses a periodic inventory system.

*Record accounts receivable and bad debts transactions; discuss statement presentation.*
*(SO 1, 2, 4) AP*

On August 31, 2008, after completing its month-end adjustments, it had accounts receivable of $742,500, a credit balance of $27,570 in Allowance for Doubtful Accounts, and bad debts expense of $85,680. In September and October, the following occurred:

September
1. Sold $546,300 of merchandise on account.
2. A total of $9,170 of the merchandise sold on account was returned. These customers were issued credit memos.
3. Collected $592,750 cash on account from customers.
4. Interest charges of $12,020 were charged to outstanding accounts receivable.
5. As part of the month-end adjusting entries, recorded bad debts expense of 2% of net credit sales for the month.

October
1. Credit sales in the month were $639,900.
2. Received $3,450 cash from a customer whose account had been written off in July.
3. Collected $585,420 cash, in addition to the cash collected in (2) above, from customers on account.
4. Wrote off $46,480 of accounts receivable as uncollectible.
5. Interest charges of $12,070 were charged to outstanding accounts receivable.
6. Recorded the year-end adjustment for bad debts. Uncollectible accounts were estimated to be 3% of accounts receivable.

### Instructions

(a) Record the above transactions and adjustments.
(b) Show how accounts receivable will appear on the October 31, 2008, balance sheet.
(c) What amount will be reported as bad debts expense on the income statement for the year ended October 31, 2008?
(d) Where are bad debts expense and interest revenue shown on the income statement?

Record receivables
transactions.
(SO 2, 3) AP

**P8–8B** Bleumortier Company has a March 31 fiscal year end. Selected transactions in the year included the following:

Jan.  2 Sold $9,000 of merchandise to Brooks Company, terms n/30.
Feb.  1 Accepted a $9,000, 3-month, 6% promissory note from Brooks Company for the balance due (see January 2 transaction). Interest must be paid monthly.
     18 Sold $4,000 of merchandise to Mathias Co., terms n/10.
Mar.  1 Collected the monthly interest payment from Brooks Company (see February 1 transaction).
      2 Accepted a $4,000, 3-month, 5.5% note from Mathias Co. for its balance due, with interest payable at maturity.
     31 Accrued interest on any outstanding notes.
Apr.  1 Collected the monthly interest payment from Brooks Company (see February 1 transaction).
May   1 Collected Brooks Company note in full (see February 1 transaction).
June  2 Mathias Co. dishonours its note of March 2. It is expected that Mathias will eventually pay the amount owed.
July 13 Sold $5,000 of merchandise to Tritt Inc. and accepted Tritt's $5,000, 3-month, 7% note for the amount due, with interest payable at maturity.
Oct. 13 The Tritt Inc. note was dishonoured (see July 13 transaction). Tritt Inc. is bankrupt and there is no hope of future settlement.

**Instructions**

Record the above transactions. (Round calculations to the nearest dollar.)

Record receivable
transactions. Show balance
sheet presentation.
(SO 1, 3, 4) AP

**P8–9B** Tardif Company adjusts its books monthly. On September 30, 2008, selected ledger account balances are as follows:

| | |
|---|---|
| Notes Receivable | $32,700 |
| Credit Cards Receivable | 16,300 |
| Interest Receivable | ? |

Notes receivable include the following:

| Issue Date | Maker | Principal | Interest | Term |
|---|---|---|---|---|
| Aug. 1, 2007 | FRN Inc. | $ 9,000 | 5.50% | 2 years |
| May 31, 2008 | IMM Ltd. | 7,500 | 5.25% | 9 months |
| Aug. 31, 2008 | DRX Co. | 6,000 | 5.00% | 2 months |
| Sept. 30, 2008 | MGH Corp. | 10,200 | 6.00% | 16 months |

Interest is payable on the first day of each month for notes with terms of one year or longer. Interest is payable at maturity for notes with terms less than one year. In October, the following transactions were completed:

Oct.  1 Received payment of the interest due from FRN Inc.
      7 Made sales of $5,800 on Tardif credit cards.
     29 Collected $4,100 of Tardif credit card receivables.
     31 Added $325 to Tardif credit card customer balances for interest charges on unpaid balances.
     31 Received notice that the DRX note had been dishonoured. (Assume that DRX is expected to pay in the future.)

**Instructions**

(a) Calculate the interest receivable at September 30, 2008.
(b) Record the October transactions and the October 31 adjusting entry for accrued interest receivable.
(c) Enter the balances at October 1 in the receivables accounts, and post the entries to all of the receivables accounts.
(d) Show the balance sheet presentation of the receivables accounts at October 31.
(e) How would the journal entry on October 31 be different if DRX were not expected to pay in the future?

**P8–10B**  Tocksfor Company's general ledger included the following selected accounts (in thousands) at September 30, 2008:

| | | | |
|---|---|---|---|
| Accounts payable | $1,436.4 | Interest revenue | $ 26.3 |
| Accounts receivable | 787.1 | Merchandise inventory | 841.2 |
| Accumulated amortization—equipment | 1,144.9 | Notes receivable—due in 2009 | 128.0 |
| Allowance for doubtful accounts | 47.2 | Notes receivable—due in 2012 | 254.8 |
| Bad debts expense | 121.7 | Prepaid expenses and deposits | 26.8 |
| Cash and cash equivalents | 787.3 | Sales | 6,087.3 |
| Cost of goods sold | 880.5 | Sales discounts | 41.7 |
| Equipment | 2,310.4 | Supplies | 29.0 |
| | | Unearned sales revenue | 75.1 |

Additional information:

1. The net realizable value of the accounts receivable was $765.9 thousand on September 30, 2007.
2. The receivables turnover was 8.3 the previous year.

**Instructions**

(a) Prepare the assets section of the balance sheet.
(b) Calculate the receivables turnover and average collection period. Compare these results to the previous year's results and comment on any trends.

**P8–11B**  Presented here is selected financial information (in millions) from the 2005 financial statements of **Rogers Communications Inc.** and **Shaw Communications Inc.**:

| | Rogers | Shaw |
|---|---|---|
| Sales | $7,482.2 | $2,209.8 |
| Allowance for doubtful accounts, Jan. 1 | 94.0 | 23.0 |
| Allowance for doubtful accounts, Dec. 31 | 98.5 | 31.9 |
| Accounts receivable balance (gross), Jan. 1 | 767.9 | 142.5 |
| Accounts receivable balance (gross), Dec. 31 | 989.2 | 146.6 |

**Instructions**

Calculate the receivables turnover and average collection period for both companies. Comment on the difference in their collection experiences.

**P8–12B**  The following ratios are available for Satellite Mechanical:

| | 2008 | 2007 | 2006 |
|---|---|---|---|
| Current ratio | 2.0 to 1 | 1.8 to 1 | 1.6 to 1 |
| Receivables turnover | 6.5 times | 7.3 times | 8.7 times |
| Inventory turnover | 6.9 times | 7.6 times | 8.5 times |

**Instructions**

(a) Calculate the collection period, days sales in inventory, and operating cycle for each year.
(b) Has Satellite Mechanical's liquidity improved or weakened over the three-year period? Explain.

# Continuing Cookie Chronicle

(*Note:* This is a continuation of the Cookie Chronicle from Chapters 1 through 7.)

Natalie has been approached by one of her friends, Curtis Lesperance. Curtis runs a coffee shop where he sells specialty coffees, and prepares and sells muffins and cookies. He is very anxious to buy one of Natalie's fine European mixers because he would then be able to prepare larger batches of muffins and cookies. Curtis, however, cannot afford to pay for the mixer for at least 30 days. He has asked Natalie if she would be willing to sell him the mixer on credit.

Natalie comes to you for advice and asks the following questions:

1. Curtis has given me a set of his most recent financial statements. What calculations should I do with the data from these statements and what questions should I ask him after I have analyzed the statements? How will this information help me decide if I should extend credit to Curtis?
2. Is there another alternative other than extending credit to Curtis for 30 days?
3. I am thinking seriously about being able to have my customers use credit cards. What are some of the advantages and disadvantages of letting my customers pay by credit card?

The following transactions occurred in June through August, 2008:

June 1 After much thought, Natalie sells a mixer to Curtis on credit, terms n/30, for $1,250 (cost of mixer $566).

   30 Curtis calls Natalie. He is unable to pay the amount outstanding for another month, so he signs a 1-month, 8.25%, note receivable.

July 31 Curtis calls Natalie. He cannot pay today but hopes to have a cheque for her at the end of the week. Natalie prepares the correct journal entry.

Aug. 10 Curtis calls again and promises to pay at the end of August, including interest for two months.

   31 Natalie receives a cheque from Curtis in payment of his balance owing plus interest outstanding.

### Instructions

(a) Answer Natalie's questions.
(b) Prepare journal entries for the transactions that occurred in June, July, and August.

## BROADENING YOUR PERSPECTIVE

# Financial Reporting and Analysis

## Financial Reporting Problem

**BYP8–1**  The receivables turnover, collection period, and operating cycle for **The Forzani Group Ltd.** were calculated in this chapter, based on the company's financial statements for the 2006 fiscal year. These consolidated financial statements are presented in Appendix A.

### Instructions

(a) Calculate Forzani's receivables turnover, collection period, and operating cycle for the 2005 fiscal year. Note that the company's accounts receivable and inventory at the end of its 2004 fiscal year amounted to $36,319 thousand and $258,816 thousand respectively.
(b) Comment on any significant differences which you observe between the ratios for 2006 (as calculated in the chapter) and 2005 (as calculated above).

## Interpreting Financial Statements

**BYP8–2**  **Suncor Energy Inc.** reported the following information (in millions) in its financial statements for the fiscal years 2003 through 2005:

|                                          | 2005    | 2004    | 2003    |
| ---------------------------------------- | ------- | ------- | ------- |
| Operating revenues (assume all credit)   | $9,749  | $8,270  | $6,329  |
| Accounts receivable (gross)              | 1,143   | 630     | 509     |
| Allowance for doubtful accounts          | 4       | 3       | 4       |
| Total current assets                     | 1,916   | 1,195   | 1,279   |
| Total current liabilities                | 1,935   | 1,409   | 1,060   |

Additional detail about Suncor's receivables includes the following:

The company has a securitization program in place to sell to a third party, on a revolving, fully serviced, and limited recourse basis, up to $340 million of accounts receivable having a maturity of 45 days or less. As at December 31, 2005, $340 million in outstanding accounts receivable had been sold under the program.

Industry averages are as follows: current ratio, 1.45:1; receivables turnover, 7.3 times; and average collection period, 50 days.

### Instructions

(a) Calculate the current ratios, receivables turnover ratios, and average collection periods for fiscal 2005 and 2004. Comment on Suncor's liquidity for each of the years and compared to the industry.

(b) In 2005, Suncor's dollar amount of its allowance for doubtful accounts was the same as it was in 2003. Comment on the relevance of this as a percentage of accounts receivable.

(c) Suncor regularly sells a portion of its accounts receivable. Comment on this practice as part of Suncor's management of its accounts receivable.

# Critical Thinking

## Collaborative Learning Activity

*Note to instructors:* Additional instructions and material for this group activity can be found on the Instructor Resource Site.

**BYP8–3** In this group activity, you will work in pairs to review the following two approaches to estimate bad debts:

1. Percentage of sales
2. Percentage of receivables

### Instructions

(a) In your pair, each select one of the above approaches. Temporarily leave your partner and join the "expert" group for that approach.

(b) In the "expert" group, use the handout given to you by your instructor and discuss your approach. Ensure that each group member thoroughly understands it.

(c) Return to your partner and explain your approach.

(d) You may be asked by your instructor to write a short quiz on this topic.

Study Aids:
Working in Groups

## Communication Activity

**BYP8–4** Toys for Big Boys sells snowmobiles, personal watercraft, ATVs, and the like. Recently, the credit manager of Toys for Big Boys retired. The sales staff threw him a big retirement party—they were glad to see him go because they felt his credit policies restricted their selling ability. The sales staff convinced management that there was no need to replace the credit manager since they could handle this responsibility in addition to their sales positions.

Study Aids:
Writing Handbook

Management was thrilled at year end when sales doubled. However, accounts receivable quadrupled and cash flow halved. The company's average collection period increased from 30 days to 120 days.

### Instructions

In a memo to management, explain the financial impact of allowing the sales staff to manage the credit function. Has the business assumed any additional credit risk? What would you recommend the company do to better manage its increasing accounts receivable?

## Ethics Case

**Study Aids:
Ethics in Accounting**

**BYP8–5**  The controller of Proust Company has completed an aging schedule, using the following percentages to estimate the uncollectible accounts: 0–30 days, 5%; 31–60 days, 10%; 61–90 days, 30%; 91–120 days, 50%; and over 120 days, 80%. The president of the company, Suzanne Bros, is nervous because the bank expects the company to sustain its current growth rate of at least 5% over the next two years—the remaining term of its bank loan. President Bros suggests that the controller increase the percentages, which will increase the amount of the required bad debts expense adjustment. The president thinks that the lower net income (because of the increased bad debts expense) will make it easier next year to show a better growth rate.

### Instructions

(a) Who are the stakeholders in this case?
(b) Does the president's request create an ethical dilemma for the controller?
(c) Should the controller be concerned with Proust Company's growth rate in estimating the allowance? Explain your answer.

---

## ANSWERS TO CHAPTER QUESTIONS

### Answers to Accounting in Action Insight Questions

#### Business Insight, p. 411

**Q:** Since the interest rates on company credit cards are so high, why don't all companies have their own credit cards?

**A:** It might sound like a great idea for a company to have its own credit card if customers are willing to pay interest rates as high as 28.8%. But if a company has its own credit card, it will have to do a credit check on each customer, keep track of all of the customer accounts, absorb any losses if a customer does not pay, and wait for customers to pay so that the cash is available for the company to use.

#### Across the Organization Insight, p. 424

**Q:** If you were a loans officer at a bank, how would you decide whether or not to make a loan to a company?

**A:** The most important thing is to decide whether or not the company will be able to repay the loan. You should find out about the company's business, about how it plans to use the money, and about how it plans to repay the money. You should also evaluate the company's past liquidity and profitability. Loans should not be given because of the political connections of the company's owners or managers.

### Business Insight, p. 429

**Q:** Why would Sears sell its credit card operations to an unrelated company?

**A:** Companies are always looking for ways to increase profits through either cutting costs or increasing revenues. Sears would have compared the amount it expects to earn in performance payments from JPMorgan Chase to what it earned from the credit card operations, and then concluded that it could earn more on the performance payments. In addition, because JPMorgan Chase already has an extensive credit card operation, it will probably be able to process and manage the credit card receivables at a lower cost than Sears.

### Answer to Forzani Review It Question, p. 412

In Note 2(h) on revenue recognition, The Forzani Group Ltd. states that it earns revenue on both sales to customers in stores and from sales to, and service fees from, franchise stores and others. Forzani also states that revenue is recognized on sales to franchise stores at the time of shipment. These sales to franchise stores are probably on credit. Forzani would therefore record a receivable from the franchise store when the merchandise is shipped.

### Answers to Self-Study Questions

1. b   2. b   3. d   4. c   5. c   6. b   7. d   8. a   9. c   10. d

Remember to go back to the Navigator Box at the beginning of the chapter to check off your completed work.